Cambridge Elements ≡

Elements in Public and Nonprofit Administration
edited by
Andrew Whitford
University of Georgia
Robert Christensen
Brigham Young University

THE COURTS AND THE PRESIDENT

Judicial Review of Presidential Directed Action

Charles Wise
The Ohio State University

Shaftesbury Road, Cambridge CB2 8EA, United Kingdom

One Liberty Plaza, 20th Floor, New York, NY 10006, USA

477 Williamstown Road, Port Melbourne, VIC 3207, Australia

314–321, 3rd Floor, Plot 3, Splendor Forum, Jasola District Centre, New Delhi – 110025, India

103 Penang Road, #05–06/07, Visioncrest Commercial, Singapore 238467

Cambridge University Press is part of Cambridge University Press & Assessment, a department of the University of Cambridge.

We share the University's mission to contribute to society through the pursuit of education, learning and research at the highest international levels of excellence.

www.cambridge.org
Information on this title: www.cambridge.org/9781009494533

DOI: 10.1017/9781009303033

When citing this work, please include a reference to the DOI 10.1017/9781009303033

First published 2024

A catalogue record for this publication is available from the British Library.

ISBN 978-1-009-49453-3 Hardback
ISBN 978-1-009-30307-1 Paperback
ISSN 2515-4303 (online)
ISSN 2515-429X (print)

The Courts and the President

Judicial Review of Presidential Directed Action

Elements in Public and Nonprofit Administration

DOI: 10.1017/9781009303033
First published online: May 2024

Charles Wise
The Ohio State University

Author for correspondence: Charles Wise, wise.983@osu.edu

Abstract: US presidents have long issued presidential directives to federal agencies to adopt and implement programs to advance presidential priorities, both pursuant to statutes passed by Congress and outside of them. From the first presidency, federal courts established their power of judicial review of such directives, but they have not always exercised that prerogative to restrict wide-ranging assertions of executive power. This examination of judicial decisions analyzes the evolution of federal judicial treatment of presidential directives and the legal bases and principles employed in federal court decisions. The Element assesses the degree to which such decisions have been restrictive or supportive of presidential directives. A more recent trend toward more restrictive principles is illuminated. Finally, the implications for presidential, congressional, and federal agency policymaking are discussed.

Keywords: presidential directives, judicial review, executive orders, agency regulations, presidents

ISBNs: 9781009494533 (HB), 9781009303071 (PB), 9781009303033 (OC)
ISSNs: 2515-4303 (online), 2515-429X (print)

Contents

1 Presidential Directives: Constitutional and Legal Considerations

Presidential Directives: Questions and Issues

Modern US presidential policymaking has increasingly deemphasized working through the congressional process in favor of presidential directives. When President Obama was frustrated in attempts to get some of his priority policy goals enacted through Congress he declared that he had a pen and a phone and he would proceed on his own. He is not the only president to circumvent Congress in favor of issuing presidential directives.

This phenomenon raises the question of how presidents are held accountable if they direct federal agencies to take steps that exceed a president's authority in the US checks and balances system. Congress has some oversight tools but few other than the appropriations process that can actually stop unwarranted presidential action. The federal courts have the power to stop action when a president's directive is challenged and they find the president's action is not legally justified. Also, courts have the power to provide justification for presidential directives when they are legally justified.

The question addressed in this Element is the extent to which the federal courts have declared support or restraint for presidential directives by modern presidents that are challenged. Relatedly, to what extent has support or restraint been declining or increasing? The degree of increase or decrease is somewhat important in addressing presidential accountability. Nonetheless, it is also instructive to examine whether the cited justifications relied upon portend more or fewer challenges to presidential directives. Both the extent of judicial challenges to presidential directives and the bases on which the judiciary either sustains or overturns such challenges have implications for public policy and administration. Administrative initiatives, management changes, and agency regulations taken pursuant to presidential directives have faced, and will continue to face, either support, restriction, or even nullification from the federal courts.

Recent presidents who have expanded the use of presidential directives have claimed broad authority for their actions, and such actions have had far wider impacts than merely affecting internal agency administrative arrangements. President Biden's COVID-19 vaccine mandates that affected the majority of American workers is a most recent example. Such widespread impacts have resulted in more challenges in the federal courts, leading the federal judiciary to deliberate over both presidents' directives and the actions of federal officials and agencies pursuant to those directives. This has led the federal courts to increasingly scrutinize these actions, and they have enunciated legal doctrines by which to assess their conformity with constitutional principles and adherence to congressionally enacted statutes.

Defenders of some presidential directives have asserted various justifications for them, including inherent or implied presidential powers contained in the US Constitution or presidential prerogatives. This Element explores the extent to which the federal courts have accepted or rejected various justifications and their rationales for doing so. It then determines the extent to which the federal courts are developing a set of principles that they can employ to assess future presidential directives. Such a set of principles could be instructive for policymakers and public administrators to weigh whether specific prospective presidential directives are likely to be sustained by the courts, and which may require reconsideration.

The term "presidential directive" is used to encompass the variety of tools presidents have utilized to direct actions by administrative agencies in order to enact their policies. Perhaps the most commonly discussed form of presidential directive is the presidential executive order (EO). While there is no mention of EOs in the US Constitution, or any constitutional or statutory definition of them, one congressional study defines them as "directives or actions by the President" that have the "force or effect of law" when "founded on the authority of the President derived from the Constitution or statute" (Committee on Government Operations, 1957, 1). However, presidents also use other tools to direct agency actions including proclamations, presidential memoranda, presidential signing statements, and national security presidential directives, among other types. One analyst identified twenty-four different types of presidential directives (Relyea, 2008). In general, the difference is typically one of form and not of substance (Branum, 2002, 140). Presidents have used a "multi-tool approach" to implement their preferred polices which can sometimes lead to patchwork policymaking (Cooper, 2001, 140).

"Presidential directive" is used here in a broad sense, in that presidents do use a variety of tools – EOs, memoranda, national security findings, and so on – to instruct agencies. Presidential directives can pertain to a variety of resultant agency actions including adoption, revoking or revising of regulations, initiation or deferment of enforcement actions, inclusion of new criteria for making agency administrative and/or policy decisions, and assuming new agency responsibilities or discontinuing old ones. It should be recognized that judicial challenges to a president's directives by opponents of the directives will often not be filed against the president directly (though some will be), but against the agency implementation pursuant to the president's directive.

The analysis in this Element will not attempt to encompass the thousands of presidential directives issued by all presidents. That endeavor would constitute a multivolume encyclopedia of such actions. The coverage here is necessarily selective and focuses primarily on presidents that have extended the reach of presidential unilateral actions to new areas of government activity, substantially altering existing ones, or extending the reach of government actions in existing programs. It also emphasizes those presidential directives that portend major policy and administrative impacts that extend beyond internal governmental processes to major groups in the public sectors of the economy, or policies and programs of state and local governments.

The Overall Structure of the Executive Power of the President Undergirding Presidential Directives

The US Constitution provides for legislative, executive, and judicial powers. However, it also includes the principles of separation of powers. The basis for the president's executive powers begins with the provisions of Article II which states, "The President shall take care that the laws are faithfully executed." From here, presidential power is then derived from other provisions in the Constitution and authorities that can reasonably be drawn from those provisions (implied powers). Other sources of presidential power include statutory grants of authority from congressional specifications in individual statutes, judicial decisions, and the requirements of national emergencies. Several presidents have asserted that their declarations rest on "inherent power" vested in the Office of the President by the Constitution (Fisher, 2015a). However, assertions of inherent power are highly contentious and have been disputed. "Presidents Truman, Nixon, and Bush II claimed the right to exercise inherent powers. On each occasion they were rebuffed by Congress, the Supreme Court, or both" (Fisher, 2015a, 298).

Presidential executive power is not unbounded but constrained by the separation of powers embodied in the Constitution. The separation of powers serves to both constrain and support the president's exercise of executive authority.

> It reinforces a president's right or duty to issue a decree, order, or proclamation to carry out a particular power that is truly committed to his discretion by the Constitution or by a lawful statute passed by Congress. On the other hand, the constitutional separation of powers cuts the other way if the president attempts to issue an order regarding a matter that is expressly committed to another branch of government; it might even render the presidential action void. Finally, separation of power principles may be unclear or ambiguous when the power is shared by two branches of government. (Gazino, 2001, 2)

Public Administration and Presidential Directives

The issue for public administration is: What are the implications of presidential directives for the position and responsibilities of federal agencies and federal administrators with regard to presidential direction? At first glance, the implications for federal administrators' decision-making may appear straightforward – the president heads the executive branch, and administrative agencies are constituent parts of the executive branch. Therefore, the responsibility of federal administrators is to do whatever the president has directed. It is not, however, that simple. In the first place, in the US Constitution the specificity of federal agency and federal administrators' responsibilities with regard to presidential authority is neither comprehensive nor explicit. This has significant implications for federal administrative decision-making.

The Constitutional Basis for Administrative Agency Action

The US Constitution does not provide much specificity when it comes to providing for administrative agencies, their powers, or the authority to direct them. It mentions them rather obliquely in Article II when setting out the appointment of administrative officers and the president's ability to demand their opinions. Article II is really devoted to the president's powers. With regard to appointments, Article II, section II states that with regard to the president's appointment powers, in addition to ambassadors, other public ministers and consuls, and judges of the Supreme Court, he can appoint "all other Officers of the United States, whose appointments are not herein provided for and who shall be established by law." However, Section II does not assign the appointment power exclusively to the president because it also states, "but the Congress may by Law vest the appointment of such inferior officers, as they think proper in the President alone, in the Courts, or in the Heads of Departments." Thus, the president is not necessarily the sole appointing authority for federal administrators.

The president's executive authority is grounded in Article II, section III, where, as noted, it provides, "he shall take care that the Laws be faithfully executed." With respect to the obligations of the administrative agencies with regard to this executive responsibility to take care that the laws are fairthfully executed, the Constitution does say all that much. Article II, section II states with regard to the president, "he may require the opinion in writing of the principal Officer in each of the executive departments, upon any subject relating to the duties of their respective offices." However, the Constitution is not then explicit about the nature and extent of the president's authority over administrative agencies. What is there beyond "requiring their opinions in writing"? Presumably, further presidential authority stems from the "take care" clause, but how far that presidential authority extends vis-à-vis the other two branches of government, and in what circumstances, is not made explicit with regard to administrative agencies.

Howell (2005) observes that: "But given the ambiguity of Article II powers and the massive corpus of law that presidents can draw upon, as well as the well-documented travails of the legislative process, the appeal of unilateral power is readily apparent. Not surprisingly, almost all the trend lines point upward" (417). Presidents, and even presidential candidates, contemplating those legislative travails have been increasingly assertive about unilateral action. When running for president, Kamala Harris (vice president, at the time of writing), discussing gun control declared, "I will give the United States Congress 100 days to pull their act together . . . and put a bill on my desk for signature. And if they do not, I will take executive action . . . There's been no action. As president, I will take action." Moe and Howell (1999) observe that because the phrases in Article II are so widely applicable to virtually everything the president might contemplate doing, their inherent ambiguity provides the opportunity for the exercise of a residuum of unenumerated power, and thus, for presidents to lay claim to what is not explicitly granted to them.

> And because the Constitution does not say precisely what the proper boundaries of their power are, and because their hold on the executive functions of government give them pivotal advantages in the political struggle, they have strong incentives to push for expanded authority by moving into grey areas of the law, asserting their rights, and exercising them – whether or not other actors, particularly Congress, happen to agree. (Moe and Howell, 1999, 856)

The US Constitution does not specify the powers and authority of federal administrative agencies and federal administrators. So, where does the authority of administrative agencies fit within the constitutional and legal structure? As John Rohr has stated,

> The powers of administrative agencies, unlike those of Congress, the President, and the Courts, are always "partial" and never "whole." They are partial, because they are exercised over a narrowly defined scope of government activity – for example tv [*sic*] licensing. Not only are their powers partial, but – unlike those of Congress, the President, and the Courts – they are formally subordinated in their entirety to one or another of the traditional branches. (Rohr, 1986, 27)

But to which branches and under what circumstances are federal administrative agencies subordinated? The Constitution does not clarify that. Thus, as I have written previously,

> by the very structure of the government that the Constitution created, while the roles of subordinate administrators begin from their position in the executive, the allocation of powers to the other branches which impact and

control administrators as well, literally put[s] them in the middle subject to the pulling and hauling of the actions by the various branches and, in turn, [makes them] participants in the pulling and hauling themselves. (Wise, 1993, 260)

In effect, decisions have to be made by federal administrators on which branch to favor in the context of particular policy disputes between the branches (Wise, 1993, 260). This overlapping authority structure which governs federal administration agencies means that presidential authority to direct agency policy and implementation actions is not unequivocal. Agencies are responsible to Congress and the federal courts as well.

Federal administrators make decisions in three major categories: (1) in proposing presidential directives, (2) in implementing presidential directives, and (3) in reacting to presidential directives.

Federal Agencies' Participation in Proposing Presidential Directives

The responsibilities of federal agencies and administrators do not merely lie in receiving and implementing presidential directives. With regard to EOs, for example, 44–49 percent are crafted entirely by agencies outside of the Executive Office of the President (Rudalevige, 2021, 203). In addition, EOs are supposed to go through the clearance process managed by the Office of Management and Budget (OMB), though not all do; one-third do not, and are produced jointly by an agency, or a small subset of agencies, along with White House staff (Rudalevige, 2021, 205).

The point of the clearance process is to identify problematic drafting demands that would prevent the EO from being effective, or provisions that would be nullified by the federal courts. Theodore Olson, head of the Justice Department's Office of Legal Counsel during the Reagan administration, stressed central clearance's ability to help the president "minimize his exposure to the type of problems which detract disproportionally from the implementation of his policy objectives" (Olson, 1983). It is apparent that President Trump's first two immigration EOs did not proceed through the complete clearance process, and both were rejected by the federal courts. Agency staff were involved with preparing the third EO and it was approved.

If an EO does go through the clearance process, agencies have to decide whether to support or oppose it and how assiduously to point out potential pitfalls. This calls for a complex understanding of the political context surrounding the order, especially if the president has spoken out about his desire to promulgate such an order.

Federal Agency Decisions in Implementing Presidential Directives

Presidents contemplating directives cannot be completely confident that their EOs will be implemented by federal agencies. "Recent years provide many examples of EOs approved with great fanfare falling short on the ground, from Obama's effort to shutter Guantanamo Bay to Trump's wall and pipeline building" (Rudalevige, 2021, 208). A career OMB administrator was quoted as observing that during his decades serving in OMB he "often found it interesting and perplexing that presidential statements through executive orders, memoranda, or other administrative actions were unknown, unrecognized, or ignored" (Rudalevige, 2021, 209). Ronald Reagan's EO 126 to regulate property takings, for example, "was heavily disliked and fought every step of the way by affected agencies" and later "for practical purposes, simply ignored" (Kennedy, 2018, 17).

It may be argued that, given the plurality of interests embedded in the various federal agencies, presidents are well advised to negotiate the field of such interests to achieve a directive that will be effectively implemented by contending agencies. Moreover, it has been argued that presidents who assume a top-down authority approach are less likely to be effective. Instead, presidents have to engage in bargaining with the agencies, which takes time and resources. Rudalevige (2021, 220) argues that presidents need to get better at bargaining.

Agency administrators need to be active participants in bargaining as well. Nonetheless, they need to be aware that achieving a deal with other agencies and the president may well not be the final word on implementation. Actions by the federal courts could modify or nullify a president's directive. Thus, even the most assiduously bargained deals within the executive branch can come apart. It is wise for administrators to remember that federal courts are not parties to bargaining with the president.

Administrators' and Officials' Reactions to Presidential Directives

Public officials and administrators making decisions about how to react to presidential directives often include state and local officials as well as federal administrators. This is because of the intergovernmental system within which so many federal programs are implemented. For example, President Trump's EO 13768 (discussed in Section 5) directed the attorney general to act against self-proclaimed sanctuary cities. It provided that local governments failing to supply information to federal immigration authorities would be ineligible to receive certain federal grants. The attorney general had to decide whether or not to proceed against such sanctuary cities, and local government officials had to decide whether to comply or challenge the order in federal court. The City of

Santa Clara and the City and County of San Francisco decided to challenge it and filed suit against the EO in federal court.

Public administrators have to gauge whether a president's EO, and also the agency regulations enacted pursuant to them, will be supported, restricted, or nullified by the federal courts and plan accordingly. For example, President Obama issued his EO Deferred Action for Parents of Americans and Lawful Permanent Residents, pursuant to which 4.3 million people would have been eligible for several federal as well as state benefits involving billions of dollars. As discussed in Section 5 (President Biden), federal courts overturned the order.

Public administrators also need to consider whether or not the advantages of a president's directive outweigh the disadvantages. For example, administrators in some states may have supported the objectives of President Obama's Clean Power Plan (discussed in Section 4) to reduce greenhouse gas emissions generated by utilities, but they also had to consider the increased electricity costs for their states, as well as how much greenhouse gas emissions would be reduced overall. They had to take into consideration as well what alterations in state regulations would be needed. Also, given that the change in utility regulation was being effected by the order of a president and not by a law, they had to consider whether the next president would reverse the order, which is precisely what occurred. Finally, administrators need to consider the potential for a presidential directive to be rejected by the courts. All these considerations go into decisions about whether to challenge, or even file, briefs in support of a challenged directive, as well as whether to set implementation plans in motion.

Legal Bases for Presidential Directives

The federal courts are increasingly being petitioned by various parties to make the call whether a presidential administration's claim of authority strikes the right balance in terms of the separation of powers under the US Constitution.

Presidents have justified their directives on various grounds. Sometimes, presidents have cited specific statutes or constitutional provisions. At other times, they have not cited any legal provision to justify their actions. At still other times, they have claimed their directives were grounded in the inherent power of the presidency. Those expressing this last claim assert that the president exercises "a narrow implied inherent power to protect the instrumentalities of government even in the absence of specific statutory authorization" (Calabresi and Yoo, 2008, 430). Some proponents of presidential inherent powers find this power anchored in the Constitution and assert, "the Executive Power Clause grants the executive power solely and exclusively to the President" (Calabresi and Saikrichna, 1994, 581). Further, they state that:

"The Constitution unambiguously gives the President the power to control the execution of all federal laws" (Calabresi and Saikrichna, 1994, 570). They also assert: "The text and the structure of Article II compels the conclusion that the President retains supervisory control over all officers exercising executive powers" (Calabresi and Rhodes, 1992, 1215). As support for this position, they observe, "As the Framers, ratifiers, ratification opponents, members of the first Congress, and President Washington understood, the Constitution grants the President authority to superintend the administration of federal law" (Calabresi and Prakash, 1994, 664). Thus, the claim is that the Article II vesting clause clearly prescribes a unitary executive department (Calabresi and Rhodes, 1992, 1192).

Other proponents, while agreeing with the theory of the unitary executive, disagree that the legal basis can be found solely in the framer's actions. Instead, Lawrence Lessig and Cass Sunstein (1994, 95–97) argue that there have been profound changes in national government since the founding of the US Constitution. These include lawmaking and law-interpreting authority, which is now concentrated in an array of regulatory agencies, and also fundamental policy decisions that are made by administrators, so that the latter are now exercising political functions. These changes risk problems. Among them are the risk of separating fundamental policy from direct political accountability, and thus the capacity for coordination and democratic control. Further, they subject administrative institutions to the perverse incentives of factions by removing the insulating arm of the president and increasing the opportunity for interest groups (Lessig and Sunstein, 1994, 98). Therefore, Lessig and Sunstein (1994, 86) argue, "Under current circumstances a strongly unitary executive is the best way of keeping faith with the most fundamental goals of the original scheme."

Justice Elena Kagan (2001, 2326) has proposed a modified unitary theory, arguing for a presumption of presidential authority over executive agencies and a presumption against such authority for independent agencies. She finds that when Congress creates an executive agency over which the president enjoys free firing authority, it creates an agency of officials that are directly subordinate to the president. As the president's subordinates, he presumably may direct these agencies in certain ways (Kagan, 2001, 2326–2327).

Opponents of the unitary executive theory argue that it contains two fallacies. First, it fails to recognize that federal administrative agencies and their officers have two kinds of duties under the Constitution – discretionary and ministerial. Discretionary duties are those that are performed as agents of the president and, as such, these agents are answerable to the president. Ministerial duties are those not to the president but to the law. Agency heads, opponents argue, have a legal obligation to carry out the functions assigned to them by Congress as enacted into federal law (Fisher, 2004, 576). Chief Justice John Marshall explained this distinction in *Marbury* v. *Madison* with respect to the obligations of the secretary of state. Marshall stated that when the secretary of state performs as "an officer of the United States," he is bound to obey the laws (5 US 137 [1803]). In this capacity, the secretary acts "under the authority of the law, and not by the instructions of the President. It is a ministerial act which the law enjoins on a particular officer for a particular purpose" (5 US 137 [1803]). On the basis of this distinction, Fisher argues that "Presidents and their Attorneys General understand that all subordinates are not directly controllable by the President. The unity of the executive branch is diminished to that extent which is substantial" (Fisher, 2010, 579).

A second fallacy, opponents assert, is that unitary executive theorists mix up the concepts of inherent and implied powers. Implied powers are reasonably drawn from express powers and are directly linked to the Constitution. Inherent powers are not drawn from express powers but inhere in the office (Fisher, 2015a, 296). As defined by *Black's Law Dictionary*, inherent means "An authority without its being derived from another ... powers over and beyond those expressly granted in the Constitution or reasonably implied from express grants" (Black, 1979, 703). Thus, implied powers are derived from the Constitution but inherent powers are not. Inherent powers appear to rely on a general claim tied to the Office of the President. Fisher (2010, 589) argues, "A constitution protects individual rights and liberties by specifying and limiting government. Express and implied powers serve that purpose. The claim of 'inherent powers' ushers in a range of vague and abstruse sources of authority. What 'inheres' in the President?" Fisher contends that much of the work by executive branch subordinates is determined by law. Administrative responsibilities such as adjudicatory functions within the executive power, for example, are off-limits to the president and are carried out to satisfy the explicit direction of Congress through statutorily assigned tasks (Fisher, 2010, 590).

Advantages and Disadvantages of Presidential Directives

In addition to the legal bases for presidential directives, the issue of effectiveness requires consideration. That is, are presidential directives an effective way to implement policy that benefits citizens and sustains democratic government?

One of the primary reasons the Founders at the Constitutional Convention decided to abandon the Articles of Confederation and adopt a new constitution was the recognition that American national government was sorely lacking in the performance of executive functions. Administration by Congress had been woefully insufficient for implementing policies to safeguard the country and assist in its development. Alexander Hamilton, one of the Founding Fathers, argued for a new presidency responsible for administering policy: "[A] feeble execution implies a feeble execution of government. A feeble execution is but another phrase for bad execution; and a government ill executed, whatever it may be in theory, must be in practice a bad government" (Hamilton, 1987, 402).

One advantage of issuing directives for presidents is that it appears to be faster than legislating. As Howell (2005) has pointed out, when presidents act unilaterally they move policy first and thereby place upon Congress and the courts the burden of revising a new political landscape. The president can issue a specific policy mandate and need not rally majorities in Congress, compromise with adversaries, or wait for some interest group to bring a case to court. Instead, when the president acts unilaterally, he acts alone. Presidents often use unilateral power to issue policies when Congress is deadlocked on an issue and the president can create a policy that otherwise would not exist at all (Howell, 2005, 421, 429; see also Lowande and Rogowski, 2021, 22). An example is Trump's EO to build a border wall. Moe and Howell (1999, 852) assert that presidents have strong incentives to push the ambiguity in the formal constitutional structure of government relentlessly – yet strategically, and with moderation, to extend their own power; the result is a slow but steady shift of the institutional balance of power over time in favor of presidents.

Some scholars point to the power of the president to effectively make and update policy that fosters popular control as a reason to support presidential directives. Justice Kagan argues that presidential leadership of administration enhances transparency, enabling the public to comprehend more accurately the sources and nature of bureaucratic power. She asserts that the presidency's unitary power structure, its visibility, and its "personality" all render the office peculiarly apt to exercise power in ways that the public can identify and evaluate. Thus, presidential leadership establishes an electoral link between the public and the bureaucracy, increasing the latter's responsiveness to the public (Kagan, 2001, 2331–2332). Relatedly, Strauss and Sunstein (1986, 190) argue that the president is electorally accountable and is the only official in government with a national constituency, which makes him uniquely well situated to design policy in a way that is responsive to the interests of the public as a whole.

Kagan (2001, 2339) also asserts that presidential control of administration means more regulatory effectiveness by providing dynamism and energy in administration which entails both the capacity and the willingness to adopt, modify, and revoke regulations expeditiously to solve national problems. The president can act without the indecision and inefficiency that often characterizes the behavior of collective entities, and can synchronize and apply general principles to agency action in a way that congressional committees, interest groups, and bureaucratic experts cannot.

Kagan further advises that presidential control increases coordination of many offices with overlapping jurisdictional authority. The president can identify and then eliminate inconsistencies and redundancies caused by such overlaps. Relatedly, the president can set administrative priorities more rationally. The president can also insist on agency adherence to general regulatory principles such as cost-effectiveness (Kagan, 2001, 2340: see also Strauss and Sunstein, 1986, 189). Nonetheless, something more than coordination and priority setting is required to implement policies. Hamilton argued that the president would bring the necessary ingredient – energy: "Energy in the executive is a leading characteristic in the definition of good government" (Hamilton, 1987, 402).

Other analysts point to the disadvantages of presidentially directed action. Some observe that it is unclear what, if any, limits exist on presidential direction of executive agencies. They point out that is unclear where to draw the line between mere policy preferences and directives contrary to enacted laws (Morgan and Barsa, 2020, 296). Presidents, acting alone, can and have directed agencies to stray from congressionally enacted statutes that specified agency procedures (Morgan and Barsa, 2020, 314). Thus, presidential directives that contradict Congress and are made without the deliberative process involved in congressional lawmaking can undermine the democratic safeguards imbued in the Constitution and in statutes such as the Administrative Procedure Act (APA). Thus, such directives may reinforce public distrust in government (Morgan and Barsa, 2020, 315). One reason for potential public distrust is that laws need to be created in a way that is predictable, transparent, and justified by the circumstances (Stack, 2015, 1987). When the public perceives that laws are created, applied, and enforced erratically, unfairly, and without sufficient justification, their faith in the rule of law is diminished (Rosenfeld, 2001, 1351). Predictable, transparent, and justified governance drives public trust, which is crucial to the continued stability of the democratic system (Robertson et al., 2016, 378). There is potential for the loss of public faith in the rule of law when presidents act on their own without the benefit of the deliberative procedures involved in either congressional lawmaking or agency rulemaking conducted in accordance with congressionally and judicially prescribed procedures. "Contrary to the APA and agency enabling acts, which provide for expert, deliberate, decision-making, agencies following presidential directions appear to make decisions more or less at the whim of the President" (Morgan and Barsa, 2020, 321).

In addition, administrative policymaking by presidential directives potentially introduces significant volatility. Given that presidential direction is generally driven by the president's political views, exactly how policies will change with each new president is not clear, and when polices rapidly change this can add instability into the administrative process (Kagan, 2001, 2315). Therefore, presidential directives can not only introduce instability by forcing agencies to vacillate wildly from one policy position to another between different presidents, but they can lead to irregularities in agency actions over the years and diminish the transparency and justification of the lawmaking process (Morgan and Barsa, 2020, 322).

Legal observers, as well as members of Congress, have been concerned about presidential directives and have seen fundamental problems with them for some time. Branum asserts:

> The Constitution does not give one individual an "executive pen" enabling that individual to single-handedly write his preferred policy into law. Despite this lack of constitutional authority, presidential directives have been increasingly used – both by Republicans and Democrats – to promulgate laws and to support public policy initiatives in a manner that circumvents the proper lawmaking body, the United States Congress. (Branum, 2002, 2)

Fisher, moreover, argues that unilateral action by EO can be damaging to presidents, private citizens, and the nation (Fisher, 2015a, 306).

2 Presidential Directives in American History

Over the years, several scholars examining decisions of the federal courts concerning challenges to presidential directives have complained about the federal courts in general, and the Supreme Court in particular, issuing decisions that have been overly deferential to presidents and insufficiently protective of the separation of powers (Fisher, 2017). That may have been generally true for a considerable period of time, with some notable exceptions, but in recent years it can be observed that the federal courts have taken a more restrictive approach.

The evolution of judicial treatment of presidential directives is laid out in this section and in those that follow. A rough summary of of the overall pattern in displayed in Table 1.

The table summarizes, for various eras, whether the federal courts' treatment of directives was generally supportive, mixed, or restrictive. It should be noted that this represents a rough characterization of broad trends. In fact, several individual presidents have experienced some directives falling in more than one category. The discussion of presidents and their directives analyzed in this section and in those that follow produce a fuller perspective of the trends and the principles employed in those decisions.

Table 1 Federal court decisions in cases challenging presidential directives

Presidents	Supportive	Mixed	Restrictive
George Washington John Adams			X
Abraham Lincoln Theodore Roosevelt Woodrow Wilson Franklin Roosevelt	X		
Harry Truman Richard Nixon Jimmy Carter Ronald Reagan George H. W. Bush William Clinton		X	
George W. Bush Barack Obama Donald Trump Joe Biden			X

George Washington (1789–1797) and John Adams (1797–1801)

Early presidents primarily used presidential directives as administrative tools (Branum, 2002, 5). Sterling (2000, 102) found that the first twenty-five presidents used EOs sparingly. Nonetheless, even at the beginning of the operation of the federal government under the US Constitution, the courts became involved in adjudicating challenges to presidents. George Washington issued an order that sparked opposition in a court when he issued a Neutrality Proclamation on April 22, 1793 which declared the neutrality of the United States in the war between Great Britain and France. The proclamation directed federal law officers to prosecute all persons who violated the order of neutrality. Gideon Henfield, a US citizen, was the prize master on a schooner commissioned by France to capture vessels on the high seas. He was charged with violating Washington's Neutrality Proclamation by taking ships belonging to Great Britain, Prussia, Sardinia, and Hungary with which the United States was at peace. Henfield was prosecuted for violating the order, but he was acquitted, because the jurors said they refused to convict anyone simply based on a presidential proclamation and not on a statute passed by Congress (Fisher, 2015, 305). And so, even in the first presidential administration, a court defended the separation of powers.

America's second president, John Adams, also faced pushback from a court over his issuing of a directive involving war powers. A law passed by Congress authorized the president to seize vessels sailing to French ports. Adams issued an order directing American vessels to seize ships sailing not only to French ports but also from them. A challenge to the order was decided by the Supreme Court. Chief Justice Marshall's opinion established the principle that a legal Act passed by Congress was superior to an EO issued by the president. Early presidents did not, however, issue many EOs. In the first 72 years of the presidency, between Washington and Buchanan, 143 executive orders were issued (Olson and Woll, 1999, 12).

Abraham Lincoln (1861–1865)

President Lincoln changed the scope and impact of presidential directives. On April 15, 1861, Lincoln issued a proclamation calling for 75,000 militia to suppress the insurrection by southern states without the involvement of Congress (Olson and Woll, 1999, 12). He also issued proclamations blocking southern ports and building warships, among other things, including an order to suspend the writ of habeas corpus (Olson and Woll, 1999, 1; Branum, 2002, 24). A writ of habeas corpus for the detained John Merryman was issued by the chief justice of the US Court of Appeals and affirmed by the Supreme Court, but Lincoln ignored the chief justice's demands (Branum, 2002, 25). Thus, the federal courts tried to constrain a Lincoln directive but were unsuccessful while the Civil War was ongoing. Also, during the war, a former member of Congress was arrested and tried before a military tribunal, and he petitioned the Supreme Court for a writ of habeas corpus. Referring to the Habeas Corpus Act, the Supreme Court concluded "it is certain that his petition cannot be brought within the 14th section of the Act, and further, that the court cannot, without disregarding the frequent decisions and interpretation of the Constitution in respect to its judicial power, originate a writ of certiorari to review or pronounce any opinion upon the proceedings of a miliary commission"; further, "Nor can it be said that the authority to be exercised by a military commission is judicial in that sense" (Ex Parte Vallandigham, 68 US 243, 251 [1863]).

When the war concluded, the Supreme Court had a different take on what the Constitution required. In Ex Parte Milligan, the court took up another case in which military authorities arrested a US citizen on charges of conspiracy; a military tribunal found him guilty and sentenced him to be hanged. Citing the US Constitution, the Supreme Court declared, "The trial of ALL crimes shall be by jury. ALL persons accused shall enjoy that privilege – and NO person shall be held to answer in any other way" (Ex Parte Milligan, 71 US 2 [1866]). The court also emphasized "it is precisely in a time of war and civil commotion that we should double the guards upon the Constitution" (Ex Parte Milligan, 71 US 2 [1866]). It concluded, "This trial was a violation of law, and no necessity could be more than a mere excuse for those who committed it" (Ex Parte Milligan, 71 US 2 [1866]).

Another case involved Lincoln's directive to place a blockade on ports in Confederate States. In Brig Amy Warwick, the Supreme Court declared, "The Constitution confers on the President the whole Executive Power" and

> he is authorized to call out the militia and use the military and naval forces of the United States in case of invasion by foreign nations, and to suppress insurrection against the government of a State or the United States .... He does not initiate the war, but is bound to accept the challenge without waiting for any special legislative authority. (Brig Army Warwick 67 US 635 [1863])

It has been pointed out that Lincoln's action with the blockade was upheld because it was limited to the domestic sphere and the court made it clear that he did not have the power to declare war against a foreign nation (Fisher, 2017, 46). Nonetheless, the court's pronouncement endorsing such strong military action employed domestically "without waiting for any special legislative authority" is surely a strong endorsement of executive power with significant effects on private property.

Theodore Roosevelt (1901–1909)

Theodore Roosevelt made extensive use of presidential directives. His predecessor, William McKinley, served for four and a half years and issued fifty-one EOs. Roosevelt served for seven years and six months and issued 1,006. Roosevelt pushed reform legislation in a number of areas, and if Congress did not act, he took action himself. Neither Congress nor the federal courts did very much to check his directives and, for the most part, he enjoyed free rein (Olson and Woll, 1999, 15).

Woodrow Wilson (1913–1921)

Woodrow Wilson used presidential directives more prolifically than his predecessors (Sterling, 2000, 102). In total, Wilson issued 1,791 EOs (Olson and Woll, 1999, 13, table 1). He declared a national emergency on February 5, 1917, two months before Congress declared war. Wilson was also the first president to create federal agencies using presidential directives and created the Food Administration, the Grain Corporation, the World Trade Board, and the Committee on Public Information. He also issued EOs to restrict radio usage, seize certain radio stations for military use, provide for collective redistribution of food for the war effort, and set prices for bituminous coal (Sterling, 2000, 103). At the time, neither Congress nor the courts did much to rein in his actions. Later, the Senate Special Committee on National Emergencies concluded that the Wilson administration was marked by the acquisition and exercise of "dictatorial powers" (Relyea, 1974, 41).

Franklin Roosevelt (1933–1945)

President Franklin Roosevelt also made extensive use of presidential directives issuing 3,723 EOs alone, more than even Wilson during World War I (Olson and Woll, 1999, 13, table 1). Roosevelt was quite public in his assertions that he would rely on his view of executive power alone if Congress did not follow his wishes. When he experienced resistance in Congress to his proposal for the Emergency Price Control Act, he declared, "In the event that the Congress should fail to act, and act adequately, I shall accept the responsibility and I will act" (quoted in Branum, 2002, 36). His first official act was to issue Proclamation 2031 which declared a national emergency and established a bank holiday, citing the authority of the Trading with the Enemy Act (TWEA) (1917) which provided no such authority and governed no transactions between US citizens absent a state of war. Franklin Roosevelt issued directives to authorize a wide variety of federal actions including seizing all gold and silver, taking the country off the gold standard, establishing a banking system based on people's debts, establishing federal control over natural resources, the social agenda and welfare, utilities, private financing, industry, labor, and transportation – and bailing out the banks (Sterling, 2000, 105). Most of these orders went unchallenged in the courts.

One order that was challenged was Executive Order 9066 which ordered the military to impose a curfew on all persons of Japanese ancestry within a designated military area – the West Coast. A case in which a citizen of Japanese ancestry was prosecuted in federal district court for violating the curfew reached the Supreme Court. The majority opinion concluded that the promulgation of the curfew order, "involved no unlawful delegation of military power" (*Hiarabayashi* v. *United States*, 320 US 81 [1943]).

Following the curfew order, the military ordered Japanese Americans to be transported to and confined in what were termed "relocation centers." When the legal challenge to the order reached the Supreme Court, the majority opinion reiterated its reasoning in the curfew case and noted, "in light of the principles we approved in the Hirabayashi case, we are unable to conclude that it was beyond the war power of Congress and the Executive to exclude those of Japanese ancestry from the West Coast at the time they did" (*Korematsu* v. *United States*, 323 US 214, 217–218 [1944]). Franklin Roosevelt claimed authority for his directive as commander in chief – essentially arguing that there was an inherent power permitting him to enable military authorities to detain a whole group of American citizens.

Another World War II case further supported Roosevelt's authority as commander in chief. This case, decided by the Supreme Court, involved the president's directive to appoint a military tribunal to try Germans who infiltrated the United States by submarine and were apprehended on American soil. Roosevelt also issued a military order appointing members of the military tribunal, the prosecutors, and the defense counsel. He also was the final reviewing authority, as after the tribunal had reached its judgment, the matter came back to him. The court observed that by the Articles of War Congress had explicitly provided that military tribunals shall have jurisdiction to try offenders or offenses against the law of war in appropriate cases, and the President as Commander in Chief had invoked that law. The court, however, in addition recognized he Prescient's inherent authority by going further to state :... and also such authority as the Constitution itself gives the Commander in Chief to direct the performance of these functions which may constitutionally be performed by the military arm of the nation in time of war (Ex parte Qurin 317 U.S. 27(1942)).

Another proclamation by President Roosevelt was issued pursuant to a statute passed by Congress that authorized the president to prohibit the sale of arms in the Chaco region of South America whenever he found that they "may contribute to the reestablishment of peace" between the belligerents (Joint Resolution to Prohibit Sale of Arms or Munitions of War in the United States Under Certain Conditions, 48 Stat. 811, ch. 365 [1934]). President Roosevelt proceeded to issue a proclamation imposing an embargo on arms shipments. Subsequently, Curtiss-Wright Corporation was indicted for conspiring to sell fifteen machine guns to Bolivia, a country engaged in armed conflict in the Chaco region. In its defense, the corporation argued that the statute effected an invalid delegation of power to the president.

The significance of the case lies not in the decision and the rationale for upholding the law and the president's proclamation; it lies in dicta, in language that was not needed or ultimately relied upon in arriving at the court's judgment. The key passage stated,

> It is important to bear in mind that we are here dealing not alone with an authority vested in the President by an exertion of legislative power, but with an authority plus the very delicate, plenary and exclusive power of the President as the sole organ of the federal government in the field of international relations – a power which does not require as a basis for its exercise an act of Congress, but which, of course, like every other governmental power, must be exercised in subordination to the applicable provisions of the Constitution. (*United States v. Curtiss-Wright Export Corp.*, 299 US 304, 319–320 [1936])

This became known as the "sole organ doctrine" and, as Fisher demonstrates, erroneous dicta tucked into a Supreme Court decision can eventually be accepted as a holding and have great influence on future constitutional doctrine (Fisher, 2016, 149). From 1936 and onwards into the early twenty-first century, the Supreme Court cited the doctrine in various other cases involving the president's powers in international relations (see Fisher, 2013). As such, the "sole organ doctrine" took on a life of its own with various administrations claiming it as authority for presidents' unilateral actions in foreign affairs.

Harry Truman (1945–1953)

President Truman followed Franklin Roosevelt's practice of extensive use of presidential directives and his claims of inherent authority as commander in chief. Truman issued 905 EOs, which was less than the number issued by Franklin Roosevelt, but more than any president prior to Theodore Roosevelt (Branum, 2002, 29). Among several EOs he issued, one seizing private businesses, EO9728, ordered the seizure of most of the bituminous coal mines so that the secretary of the interior could negotiate a contract with the United Mine Workers union. The Supreme Court refused a challenge to the order finding that the seizure was an "urgent function of government" and that the government was "exercising a sovereign function" (*United States* v. *United Mine Workers of America* 330 US 258, 298 [1947]). This "urgent function of the government" argument is essentially an inherent power rationale.

In *Youngstown Sheet and Tube* v. *Sawyer*, Truman's issued a directive to seize eighty-seven major steel companies. The administration's claim for the source of authority for his order was the president's authority as commander in chief – identical to the claim Roosevelt made. The decision on the legal challenge in the federal district court was affirmed; the judge ruled that the seizure was illegal and declared that there was no express or implied constitutional authority for it (103 F. Supp. 569, 573 [D.D.C. 1952]). The Supreme Court sustained the lower court's ruling. In addressing the administration's claim that the president had authority as commander in chief, the majority declared, "We cannot with faithfulness to our constitutional system hold that the Commander in Chief of the Armed Forces has the ultimate power as such to take possession of private property in order to keep labor disputes from stopping production. This is a job for the Nation's lawmakers, not for its military" (*Youngstown Sheet and Tube* v. *Sawyer*, 343 US 579, 587 [1952]).

It is true that Truman's steel company seizure order was the first EO to be overturned in its entirety (Branum, 2002, 30). However, the decision did not constitute a fundamental break with the federal court's affirmation of presidential directives. The decision was compromised by several concurring opinions, "often giving a green light to independent presidential power unchecked by the judiciary" (Fisher, 2017, 120). Writing fifty years later, Devins and Fisher

(2002, 756) observed, "In the years since Youngstown, judicial pronouncements relating to war powers have diminished to the point of being nonexistent" (see also Entin, 1997).

Richard Nixon (1969–1973)

A number of cases that were decided by the federal courts during the Nixon administration concerned challenges to Nixon's decisions in the conduct of the Vietnam War. These challenges were largely unsuccessful. A series of decisions by the Second Circuit Court of Appeals illustrates the difficulties the plaintiffs had in getting the court to declare the president's decisions invalid.

In *Berk* v. *Laird,* a army soldier challenged the orders he received ordering him to go to South Vietnam, arguing that the executive officials who signed his orders exceeded their authority by commanding him to participate in military activity that was not properly authorized by Congress. The court declared that since Congress had passed the Gulf of Tonkin Resolution and had implicitly, through appropriations and other acts, supported the war over the years, it would be difficult for the plaintiff to suggest a set of manageable standards and escape the conclusion that his claim was a political issue, which Congress and the president should decide through political means (*Berk* v. *Laird*, 429 F 2d 306 [1970]).

In *Orlando* v. *Laird*, army draftees asked the federal court to enjoin the secretary of defense and other officials who had signed their deployment orders from enforcing them, contending that they had exceeded their constitutional authority by ordering them to participate in a war that had not been properly authorized by Congress. Similar to its pronouncement in *Berk*, the Second Circuit cited the Gulf of Tonkin Resolution, Congress's appropriation of billions of dollars to carry out military operations in Southeast Asia, and its extension of the Selective Service Act as evidence that there was an abundance of continuing mutual participation in the prosecution of the war.

In *Da Costa* v. *Laird,* another draftee challenged the authority of executive officials to enforce orders sending him to Vietnam, arguing that Congress had never declared war against North Vietnam and that the Gulf of Tonkin Resolution had been repealed by Congress. The court declared that by extending the Selective Service Act and appropriating billions of dollars to carry out military operations, Congress had acted to ratify and approve the measures taken by the executive, even in the absence of the Gulf of Tonkin Resolution.

In *Holtzman* v. *Schlesinger*, congressional representative Elizabeth Holmes asked the court to enjoin the secretary of defense from further participation in military activities in Cambodia. The Second Circuit Court declared, "These are precisely the questions of fact involving military and diplomatic expertise not vested in the judiciary, which make the issue political and thus beyond the competence of that court or this court to determine" (*Holtzman* v. *Schlesinger*, 484 F 2d 1309 [1973]).

As the series of Vietnam War cases illustrates, until this point the courts had demonstrated a tendency to stay out of disputes involving the president directing miliary action, largely declaring that weighing the factors involved were beyond the capacity of the judiciary to assess, and also citing concerns regarding the separation of powers. The Supreme Court's political question doctrine was repeatedly employed to deny plaintiffs a full hearing on the merits of such cases involving military deployments. This was in keeping with the court's disposition, as discussed with regard to earlier cases, to accord the president significant primacy in the conduct of foreign and defense policy until this point in time.

The Supreme Court was less approving of a claim by the Nixon administration that the president's power to protect national security was sufficient to justify electronic surveillance of citizens accused of conspiracy to destroy government property. In *United States* v. *United States District Court*, three defendants were charged with conspiracy to destroy government property, and one of them was charged with the dynamite bombing of an office of the Central Intelligence Agency in Ann Arbor, Michigan. During pretrial proceedings, the defendants moved to compel the government to disclose certain surveillance information and to conduct a hearing to determine whether the information "tainted" the evidence on which the indictment was based. The government argued that the surveillance was lawful, though conducted without prior judicial approval, as a reasonable exercise of the president's power (exercised through the attorney general) to protect national security.

The government's argument reflected some of the courts' previous reasoning about judicial capacity in military operations – that, as a practical matter, courts would have neither the knowledge nor the techniques necessary to determine whether there was probable cause to believe that surveillance was necessary to protect national security. In this case, however, the court did not accept the argument that internal security matters are too subtle and complex for judicial evaluation, and stated that it did not believe prior judicial approval would fracture the secrecy essential to official intelligence gathering. The court declared that a warrant application involves no public or adversary proceedings: it is an *ex parte* request before a judge. Therefore, the court concluded that judicial approval is required prior to initiating a search or surveillance (*United States* v. *United States District Court*, 407 US 297 [1972]).

Thus, the government's rationale of claiming the president's national security powers extended to internal security and provided him with wide discretion aside from judicial scrutiny failed. The Nixon administration failed again in its bid to garner presidential discretion over the allotment of funds that Congress had authorized. Nixon, like other presidents, was frustrated by his inability to reduce the distribution of funds that he thought were excessive or wasteful. Presidents, unlike many state governors, do not have the power of the line-item veto which allows them to excise particular spending items in large multi-program appropriation bills. Nixon tried to achieve his goals on spending in another way – through the allotment process that follows the completion of appropriation laws. He tried to reduce allotments for several programs, but was sued many times. Unfortunately for him, he lost almost all of about eighty law suits in the lower courts (Fisher, 1975). One case made it to the Supreme Court. The case of *Train* v. *New York* involved a presidential claim of discretion to provide less funds than Congress had authorized under the Federal Water Control Act Amendments of 1972, which provided a program for controlling water pollution. Congress had passed the law over President Nixon's veto.

President Nixon sent a letter directing the Environmental Proterction Agency administrator not to allot to states the maximum amounts provided in the law, and instead to allot no more than $2 billion of the amount authorized for the fiscal year 1973 and no more than $3 billion of the amount authorized for fiscal year 1974. The administrator issued regulations stating, in accordance with the President's directive, that he was allotting sums not exceeding $2 billion and $3 billion for the fiscal years 1973 and 1974, respectively. The City of New York and other municipalities brought a suit seeking a judgment against the administrator, declaring that he was obligated to allot to states the full amount authorized by the law.

The Supreme Court disagreed and found that the legislation was intended to provide a firm commitment of substantial sums within a relatively limited period of time in an effort to achieve an early solution of what was deemed an urgent problem. The court opined, "We cannot believe that Congress at the last minute scuttled the entire effort by providing the Executive with the seemingly limitless power to withhold funds from allotment and obligation" (*Train* v. *New York*, 420 US 35 ([1975]). Therefore, the court concluded that the president's directive and the administrator's consequent withholding of authorized funds could not be squared with the statute.

3 Presidents Jimmy Carter, Ronald Reagan, George H. W. Bush, and William Clinton

Jimmy Carter (1977–1981)

Executive orders that started under President Carter and were continued and added to by President Reagan concerned the president's power to block transfer of property to Iran pursuant to executive agreements with that country. Thus, the case involved the power of the president to direct international relations.

On November 4, 1979, the American Embassy in Tehran was seized and American diplomatic personnel were captured and held hostage. President Carter, acing pursuant to the International Emergency Economic Powers Act (IEEPA) (91 Stat. 1626 [1977]), declared a national emergency and issued EO 12170 blocking removal or transfer of "all property and interests in property of the Government of IRAN, its instrumentalities and controlled entities, and the Central Bank of Iran."

On January 20, 1979, the Americans held hostage were released by Iran pursuant to an agreement between the United States and Iran. The agreement stated that it was the purpose of the United States and Iran to terminate all litigation between each government, and each country's nationals, and to bring about the settlement and termination of all such claims through binding arbitration. Under the agreement, the United States was obligated to terminate all legal proceedings in US courts involving claims by US persons and institutions against Iran and its state enterprises.

On January 19, 1981, President Carter issued a series of EOs implementing the terms of the agreement (EOs 12276–12285), which revoked all licenses permitting the exercise of any right, power, or privilege with regard to Iranian funds, securities, or deposits and nullified all non-Iranian interests in such assets. On February 24, 1981, (new) President Reagan issued EO 12294 ratifying Carter's EOs; he also suspended all claims which may have been presented and provided that such claims would have no legal effect in any action then pending in any court of the United states.

A company, Danes and Moore, filed an action requesting declaratory and injunctive relief against the United States, and the secretary of the treasury, to prevent enforcement of the EOs and the Treasury Department regulations implementing the agreement with Iran. The company alleged that the actions of the president and the treasury secretary were beyond their statutory and constitutional powers, and were unconstitutional to the extent that they adversely affected the company's final judgment against the government of Iran and the country's Atomic Energy Organization.

The Supreme Court referred to the "sole organ doctrine" – "the very delicate, plenary and exclusive power of the President as the sole organ of the federal government in the field of international relations – a power which does not require a basis for its exercise an act of Congress" (*Dames & Moore* v. *Regan*, 453 US 654, 660 [1981]). The court stated that President Carter had cited five sources of express or inherent power, but in its argument the government principally relied upon the IEEPA as authorization for these actions and contended that the acts of nullifying the attachments and ordering the transfer of frozen assets were specifically authorized by the plain language of the statute. The court agreed and declared,

"The language of the IEEPA is sweeping and unqualified. It provides broadly that the President may void or nullify the 'exercising by any person of any right, power, or privilege with respect to any property in which any foreign country has any interest'" (*Dames and Moore* v. *Regan*, 453 US 654 [1981]).

The Supreme Court stated "where as here, the settlement of claims has been determined to be a necessary incident to the resolution of a major foreign policy dispute between our country and another, and where, as here, we can conclude that Congress acquiesced in the President's action, we are not prepared to say that the President lacks the power to settle such cases" (453 US 687). Thus, the court continued to exhibit considerable deference to the president's power in matters of international relations. Nonetheless, it was not an unbounded deference. The court carefully documented congressional involvement in both adopting the statute undergirding the president's action and its acquiescence in presidents exercising executive authority in settling such claims. It left the door open to challenges if a president overreached and tried to stretch the statute too far.

Ronald Reagan (1981–1989)

President Reagan also acted in the domestic arena. He issued EOs to change the process that federal departments and agencies used for proposing and adopting new regulations. Reagan was not the first to initiate change in federal regulation. President Carter undertook some initiatives with respect to regulatory reform as well, such as requirements for agencies to publicly disclose their annual regulatory agenda. He also made major changes in the regulation of transportation industries. As McGarity (1986, 271) has discussed, during the 1960s and 1970s Congress had passed a wide variety of social reform laws and federal agencies promulgated many regulations to implement them. McGarity reported that the calls for regulatory reform in the late 1970s and early 1980s reflected a feeling that the means the agencies used to implement this legislation had become too intrusive.

In 1981, Reagan issued two EOs to provide for more centralized reviews of proposed regulations. Executive Order 12291 provided that, "to the extent permitted by law," regulatory action should not be taken by agencies unless they could demonstrate that the potential benefits outweigh the costs. Further, before finally promulgating "major rules" agencies were required to prepare "draft and final regulatory impact analyses" (RIAs), discussing the costs and benefits of the regulatory initiative, and the analysis had to be submitted to OMB for review and approval. If the final RIA was not approved, the agency was explicitly authorized to go forward with promulgating but should explain its differences with OMB (3 C.F.R. 127 [1982]). However, at the draft stage of rulemaking there was no statement that the agency could go forward without

OMB approval. While the ultimate power of final approval remained with the agency head, as a practical matter it was unlikely that an agency would issue a regulation without OMB approval (Strauss and Sunstein, 1986, 186).

In 1981, Reagan also issued EO 12498 which established a regulatory planning process to ensure the development and publication of any annual regulatory programs. Every agency had to submit a "draft regulatory program" to OMB for "all significant regulatory actions of the agency, planned or underway" to be undertaken in the next year. The order authorized the director of OMB to review the draft program for consistency with administration policy (50 Fed. Reg. 1036 [1985]). To some extent, it built upon and reflected the Carter program for annual public disclosure.

Strauss and Sunstein (1986, 187) argued that the orders represented an effort to deal with the general problem of uncoordinated and insufficiently accountable administrative decisions. This rationale largely reflects Kagan's (2001) argument, discussed earlier, that the president is in the best position to harmonize regulatory programs and actions from disparate agencies. However, agency actions pursuant to the EOs did not go unchallenged in the courts. While the cases did not result in the courts declaring the EOs unlawful, they had the effect of placing boundaries on the power of OMB to delay and change regulations.

In *National Resources Defense Council (NDRC)* v. *US EPA*, the NDRC sought a review for the procedures EPA used in deferring indefinitely the effective date of a set of amendments to regulations issued under the Clean Water Act, which deal with the discharge of toxic pollutants into publicly owned treatment works. A section of Reagan's EO 12291 requiring a cost–benefit analysis specified that agencies should suspend or postpone the effective dates of all major rules that they had promulgated in final form as of the date of the issuance of the order, but which had not yet become effective. Subsequently, and pursuant to the EO, the EPA administrator signed an order eliminating the effective date of the amendments (March 30, 1981) and postponing them indefinitely.

The NDRC filed suit seeking review of the EPA's action in deferring the amendments indefinitely without holding an APA notice and comment period. Subsequently, the EPA decided to terminate the indefinite postponement of the amendments and announced that they would become effective on January 31, 1981. At the same time, the EPA proposed to further suspend the amendments and invited comment on whether their effective date (or specific portions of them) should be further postponed. Thus, the EPA treated the further postponement of the amendments as a rule subject to the rulemaking provisions of the APA, even though it did not treat the initial postponement as a rule requiring the procedure.

The Court of Appeals found that the EPA could have complied with both the APA and EO 12291. It stated that the conclusion was supported by the EPA's action on October 13, 1981 when the EPA published a "final rule" terminating the indefinite postponement and a "proposed rule" proposing a future postponement, thus publishing the final rule terminating the postponement before the RIA required by the EO had been prepared. The court ruled that the indefinite postponement required notice and comment procedures prior to becoming effective (*National Resources Defense Council* v. *U.S. EPA*, 683 F 2d 753, 766 [1982]). As a result, the court granted the NDRC's petition and remanded the case to the EPA with instructions to reinstate all of the amendments effective from March 31, 1981. Thus, while the court did not decide to invalidate the EO or the obligation of the agency to work within its confines, it did insist that the agency follow the procedures of the APA.

Another case pertaining to delay of the issuance of regulations involved the Occupational Safety and Health Administration (OSHA). The Public Citizen Health Research Group sued alleging that OSHA had unreasonably delayed the promulgation of Short-Term Exposure Limit (STEL) regulations for the toxin ethylene oxide. After extensive public hearings, OSHA had been ready to issue a final rule on June 14, 1984. In compliance with EO 12291, OSHA sent the final rule to OMB for approval. However, OMB did not approve it, objecting to OSHA's inclusion of the STEL, primarily on the ground of cost-effectiveness. Then, OSHA issued a final rule which did not include STELs. The Supreme Court had previously determined that OSHA's decision to forgo a STEL did not have adequate support in the rulemaking record. It considered OSHA's failure to issue even a notice of proposed regulation in the nine months between issuance of the court's mandate and the filing of the motion then under review, and declared OSHA's action an unreasonable delay under the APA. The court noted that OSHA's regulations, first proposed in 1982, were not final by 1987, despite its repeated orders and exhortations. The OSHA informed the court that the final STEL regulations would not be issued until March 1988.

The court did observe that OSHA had decided in good faith that the record required supplementation on the issue of the public health necessity of the STEL and, viewed fairly, the court's earlier mandate did not preclude such supplementation. To the contrary, the court declared that it had specifically instructed OSHA to examine the STEL point thoroughly. The court also opined that it should intervene to override agency priorities and timetables only in the most egregious of cases. It observed that OSHA had presented to it a specific timetable that showed that a final rule would be issued in March 1988, and that it could not find any specific aspect of the proposed rulemaking schedule that was impermissibly slow in light of the complexity of the health questions involved and OSHA's limited resources.

Both the EPA and the OSHA cases demonstrate that the federal courts were not necessarily finding constitutional faults with the EOs themselves. They did make it clear, however, that the EOs would not be allowed to supersede existing statutes, and they were going to be watchful that OMB's actions did not serve to abridge or delay what the statutes mandated. The court's actions emphasized that the APA's requirements would be enforced and the agency would be expected to follow them, regardless of the mandate of the president's directive.

George H. W. Bush (1989–1993)

In 1990, a group of congressional representatives challenged President George H. W. Bush in federal court over his ordering of US troops to Saudi Arabia. On August 2, 1990, Iraq invaded Kuwait and President Bush sent US military forces to Saudi Arabia to deter Iraqi aggression and defend Saudi Arabia. On November 8, 1990, Bush substantially increased the troop level, stating that the objective was to provide an adequate offensive military option should that be necessary to achieve such goals as the withdrawal of Iraqi forces from Kuwait. In *Dellums* v. *Bush*, fifty-three members of the House of Representatives filed suit and requested an injunction directed to the president to prevent him from initiating an offensive attack against Iraq without first securing a declaration of war or other explicit congressional authorization for such action.

The Department of Justice put forth a number of arguments in defense of the president's action. Among these were that the complaint represented a nonjusticiable political question beyond the capacity of the courts and that the issue of the proper allocation of warmaking powers between the two branches was not ripe for decision. With regard to the first argument, it was the department's position that the constitutional provisions regarding warmaking – Article I regarding Congress's power to declare war and Article II regarding the power of the president as commander in chief – rendered it impossible to isolate the war-declaring power and that harmonization of war provisions is a political rather than a legal question. Thus, the department argued that deciding the issue was outside the competency of the court. In short, the department relied upon the political question doctrine.

The US District Court for the District of Columbia found that the department's claim was far too sweeping to be accepted. It declared:

> If the Executive had the sole power to determine that any particular offensive military operation, no matter how vast, does not constitute war-making, but only an offensive military attack, the congressional power to declare war will

> be at the mercy of a semantic decision by the Executive. Such an "interpret-
> ation" would evade the plain language of the Constitution and it cannot stand.
> (*Dellums* v. *Bush*, 752 F Supp. 1141, 1145 ([1991])

The court went on to find that congressional approval is required if Congress desires to become involved (752 F Supp. 1145). It affirmed the proposition that courts do not lack the power and ability to make a factual and legal determination of whether the nation's military actions constitute war for purposes of the constitutional War Clause (752 F Supp. 1146). Thus it rejected the government's assertion that the issue was beyond the competence and capabilities of federal courts.

The court found, however, that the doctrine of ripeness constituted an obstacle for the plaintiffs. In the first place, the court declared that it would have been premature and presumptuous for it to render a decision on the issue of whether a declaration of war was required at that time, when Congress itself had provided no indication as to whether it deemed such a declaration either necessary, on the one hand, or imprudent, on the other (752 F Supp. 1150). The House of Representatives Democratic caucus had passed a resolution stating that the president must first seek authorization from Congress, unless American lives were in danger. However, such a resolution on behalf of a minority in one house in Congress, and representing a caucus of one party, does not represent the entire Congress and provide the necessary indication.

Second, regarding the criteria to assess whether a case is ripe for judicial decision, the court endorsed a criteria proposed by former Supreme Court Justice Powell and adopted by several lower courts. That is, "a dispute between Congress and the President is not ready for judicial review unless and until each branch has taken action asserting its constitutional authority" (752 F Supp. 1150). Accordingly, the court concluded, "In short, unless the Congress as a whole, or by a majority, is heard from, the controversy here cannot be deemed ripe; it is only if the majority of the Congress seeks relief from an infringement on its constitutional war-declaration power that it may be entitled to receive it" (752 F Supp. 1151). The court also observed that diplomatic meetings were scheduled between the Iraqi foreign minister and the US secretary of state that could result in a diplomatic solution, and so it seemed that the executive had not shown at that time a commitment to a definite course of action sufficient to support the view that the case was ripe for decision by the court. Thus, the court was not foreclosing the opportunity for the plaintiffs to pursue their challenge later if the situation changed and they could get a majority of both houses of Congress to join them.

The court's decision on the issue of ripeness illustrates the difficulty a group of congressional representatives faces when they challenge a president's directive involving actions in military conflicts. The courts are reluctant to enter into interbranch conflicts unless Congress as a whole has acted to contain the president.

Notwithstanding the court's decision in denying the injunction, and whether or not President Bush's decision was influenced by the court and the potential for future litigation challenging his action, he did ask Congress to pass legislation in support of his policy and, on January 12, 1991, Congress passed legislation supporting his policy in the Persian Gulf (Fisher, 2017, 216).

William Clinton (1993–2001)

Several analysts have concluded that President Clinton was very aggressive in using presidential directives. "President Clinton perhaps used his powers more expansively than any president to date" (Branum, 2002, 34–35). "Clinton's agency directives sought to influence not just the process, as Reagan's directives had, but the substance of agency regulations. Indeed, Clinton's orders sometimes sought to replace the legislative process after Congress failed to pass the same or similar measures that Clinton wanted to impose" (Morgan and Barsa, 2020, 299). "Yet Clinton has repeatedly used executive orders, proclamations, and other 'presidential directives' to exercise legislative powers the Constitution vests in Congress or with the states" (Olson and Woll, 1999, 2). Almost reprising Franklin Roosevelt's words, Clinton publicly stated that he was going to continue to act on his own authority: "Congress has a choice to make in writing this chapter of our history. It can choose partisanship, or it can choose progress. Congress must decide ... I have a continuing obligation to act, to use the authority of the presidency and the persuasive power of the podium to advance America's interest at home and abroad" (Clinton, 1998, 1329). Clinton's adviser Paul Begala observed of Clinton's use of presidential directives that it was "Stroke of the pen. Law of the Land. Kind of Cool" (Bennet, 1998, 10).

Branum (2002) concludes that Clinton may have issued more controversial orders than any president in recent memory. She suggests that two characteristics of his orders perhaps made them more problematic than those of many of his predecessors: "First, he often used his power to make policy decisions that should have been left to the legislature ... Second, and more troubling, was his tendency to use presidential directives to implement initiatives that had failed to pass Congress" (38).

One of Clinton's EOs illustrates the tendency that Branum describes. It was an attempt to change the law in the area of labor relations and reverse the action of the Supreme Court. In 1938, in interpreting the National Labor Relations Act

(NLRA), the court had held that, during strike action, an employer may protect their business by hiring replacement workers and may refuse to discharge such workers later if the strikers want to return. Congress had considered and rejected legislation to amend the NLRA to prohibit employers from hiring permanent striker replacements in 1990, 1991, 1992, and 1994. Clinton issued EO 12954 which provided that federal contractors should not contract with employers that permanently replaced lawfully striking workers. The secretary of labor was charged with implementing the order. He was empowered to terminate a contract if he found that a contractor had permanently replaced lawfully striking workers, unless the head of the contracting agency objected. Pursuant to the order, the secretary of labor issued final implementing regulations.

In *Chamber of Commerce of the United States* v. *Reich*, the Chamber of Commerce and other litigants filed suit seeking declaratory and injunctive relief against the secretary of labor's enforcement of the EO, alleging that it was contrary to the NLRA, the Procurement Act, and the US Constitution. The administration claimed that there were no judicially enforceable limitations on presidential actions, besides claims that run afoul of the Constitution or which contravene direct statutory prohibitions, so long as the president states that he has acted pursuant to a federal statute. The administration asserted that he had acted pursuant to the Procurement Act. The Court of Appeals first considered whether the case, involving a challenge to an EO, was subject to judicial review. After reviewing the findings in a series of previous cases, the court concluded, "The message of this line of cases is clear enough: courts will ordinarily presume that Congress intends the executive to obey its statutory commands and accordingly, that it expects the courts to grant relief when an executive agency violates such a command" (*Chamber of Commerce of the United States* v. *Reich*, 74 F 3d 1322, 1327 ([1996]).

The court went further and opined, "That the 'executive's' action here is essentially that of the President does not insulate the entire executive branch from judicial review. We think it is now well established that review for the legality of Presidential action can ordinarily be obtained in a suit to enjoin the officers who attempt to enforce the President's directive" (74 F 3d 1327). Thus, the court rejected the administration's assertion of the unreview ability by courts of the president's action.

As to the statutory basis for Clinton's directive, the court found that the Procurement Act was a more general statute, and the NLRA was a more specific act governing labor relations, so that according to the canons of statutory interpretation a more specific statute takes precedence over a more general one. So, the court found that the NLRA governed this case. It concluded that not only would the EO and the secretary of labor's regulations have a substantial impact on American corporations, but it appeared that the secretary's regulations promised direct conflict with the NLRA (74 F 3d 1327). The court concluded "that the Executive Order is regulatory in nature and is pre-empted by the NLRA which guarantees the right to permanent replacements" (74 F 3d 1327). Clinton became only the second president to have an EO struck down in its entirety.

Another directive by President Clinton involving the line-item veto was invalidated by the Supreme Court. Clinton acted pursuant to the Line Item Veto Act (110 Stat. 1200). The Act gave the president the power to cancel in whole three types of provisions that had already been signed into law: (1) any dollar amount of discretionary budget authority; (2) any item of new direct spending; (3) any limited tax benefit. Clinton exercised his authority under the Act to cancel one provision of the Balanced Budget Act of 1997 and two provisions of the Taxpayer Relief Act, also of 1997. The City of New York sued to vindicate its interest in the Balanced Budget Act, and a farmer's cooperative sued to vindicate its interest under the Taxpayer Relief Act.

The Supreme Court observed that the president's two actions prevented sections of the two statutes from having legal force or effect (*Clinton* v. *City of New York*, 524 US 417, 435 [1998]). The court declared "There is no provision in the Constitution that authorizes the President to enact, to amend, or to repeal statutes" (524 US 438). It claimed that abundant historical materials support the conclusion that the power to enact statutes "may only be exercised in accord with a single, finely wrought and exhaustively considered procedure" (524 US 438). The court further observed that whenever the president cancels an item of new direct spending, he is rejecting the policy judgment made by Congress, relying on his own policy judgment, and not observing the procedures set out in Article I of the US Constitution (524 US 442). It concluded, "If the Line Item Veto Act were valid, it would authorize the President to create a different law – one whose text was not voted on by either House of Congress or presented to the President for his signature" (524 US 443). Finally, the court declared, "Although Congress presumably anticipated that the President might cancel some of the items in the Balanced Budget Act and the Taxpayer Relief Act, Congress cannot alter the procedures set out in Article I, without amending the Constitution" (524 US 444). The court thus invalidated both the Line Item Veto Act and Clinton's action pursuant to it. As such, it was indicating that constitutional provisions would be its touchstone, and even if the executive and the legislature were in agreement on an action that, in the court's view, violated the Constitution, it would nonetheless step in and invalidate it.

Finally, President Clinton directed that military forces be used in operations in a number of countries including Iraq, Somalia, Haiti, Bosnia, Afghanistan,

Sudan, and Serbia and Kosovo. He did not have statutory authority for any of these decisions. Instead, he relied upon UN Security Council Resolutions, the support of NATO allies, and claims of broad constitutional authority over foreign affairs and as commander in chief (Fisher, 2017, 221).

In 1999, a number of congressional representatives led by Tom Campbell sued, claiming the president violated the War Powers Resolution and the War Powers Clause of the Constitution by issuing an EO directing US military participation in the NATO campaign in Yugoslavia. The Court of Appeals for the District of Columbia Circuit questioned whether congressmen have standing in federal court to challenge the lawfulness of actions of the executive, and observed that Congress could have passed a law forbidding the use of US forces in the Yugoslav campaign and that there had, in fact, been a measure voted upon requiring the withdrawal of US troops but it had been defeated. It also observed that Congress could have cut off funds for military participation in the conflict, but even though there was an effort to do so, it failed, and appropriations were authorized. The court concluded that congressmen may not challenge the president's warmaking powers in federal court (*Campbell* v. *Clinton*, 203 F 3d 19 [2000]). Once again, a federal court expressed its refusal to consider a claim against a presidential directive brought by a minority of congressional representatives, and indicated that action by the whole Congress was necessary.

4 Presidents George W. Bush and Barack Obama

George W. Bush (2001–2009)

The priorities of the George W. Bush administration were fundamentally shifted by the September 11, 2001 terrorist attacks on the United States by Al-Queda terrorists, which killed 3,000 Americans. The focus of the administration largely moved from domestic issues to prosecuting the war on terror to protect the country. Congress took action by passing the Authorization for Use of Military Force (AUMF) (115, Stat. 224 [2001]), which authorized the President to "use all necessary and appropriate force against those nations, organizations, or persons he determined planned, authorized, committed or aided the September 11 attackers."

After the resolution was passed, President Bush ordered military action in Afghanistan. The administration was determined to use the power of the presidency to counter the terrorist threat. Vice President Dick Cheney played a leading role in exerting executive power regarding anti-terrorism operations, and had been a leading voice in the administration for restoring what he saw as a diminished power of the presidency (Biskupic, 2009, 323).

During operations, the US military captured various individuals who were accused of taking part, in some manner, in the 9/11 attacks, or who had attacked American forces. The capture of individuals whom the military deemed threats pursuant to the AUMF became the subject of several federal court cases that further defined the powers of the executive and Congress with respect to foreign and defense policy and management.

Among the individuals captured in Afghanistan by the military was Yaser Esan Hamdi, who was born in Louisiana and had, by 2001, moved to Afghanistan. He was captured and initially detained in Afghanistan, transferred to Guantanamo Bay (Cuba), and ultimately transferred to a brig in Charleston, South Carolina. Hamdi's father filed a petition for a writ of habeas corpus in federal district court alleging that the government had detained his son without access to legal counsel or notice of any charges, or access to an impartial tribunal. The government contended that Hamdi was an enemy combatant and that his status as a combatant justified holding him in the United States indefinitely – without formal charges or proceedings – unless and until it made the determination that access to counsel or further process was warranted.

The Supreme Court first took up the question of whether the executive has the authority to detain citizens who qualify as "enemy combatants." The government maintained that Hamdi was being legitimately detained pursuant to an act of Congress – the AUMF. The court agreed (*Hamdi* v. *Rumsfeld*, 542 US 507, 515 [2004]).

The second issue that the court considered was the process that Hamdi was due once he had been detained. The government contended that further factual exploration was unwarranted in light of the extraordinary constitutional interests at stake. Specifically, the government argued that respect for the separation of powers and the limited institutional capacity of courts in matters of military decision-making in connection with an ongoing conflict ought to eliminate entirely any individual probes, thus restricting the courts to investigating only whether legal authorization existed for the broader detention scheme. It was essentially an argument resting on the president's powers as commander in chief. The government asserted that courts, at most, should weigh whether it had some evidence that the person was an enemy combatant. The Supreme Court rejected the government's argument and held that "a citizen detainee seeking to challenge his classification as an enemy combatant must receive notice of the factual basis for his classification and afforded an opportunity to rebut the Government's factual assertions before a neutral decisionmaker" (542 US 532). The court took pains to assert the role of the courts in declaring, we necessarily reject the Government's assertion that separation of powers principles mandate a heavily circumscribed role of the courts in such circumstances. Indeed, the position that the courts must forgo an examination of the individual case and focus exclusively on the legality of the broader detention scheme cannot be mandated by any reasonable view of separation of powers, as this approach only serves to condense power into a single branch of government. We have long since made clear that a state of war is not a blank check for the President when it comes to the rights of the Nation's citizens. (542 US 536)

The court cited its decision in *Youngstown Sheet and Tube* during the Truman administration (discussed in Section 2) in making this declaration. It went on to emphasize, "Whatever power the United States Constitution envisions for the Executive in its exchanges with other nations or with enemy organizations in times of conflict, it most assuredly envisions a role for all three branches when individual liberties are at stake" (542 US 536). In essence, the court rejected the rationale of the "sole organ doctrine," that the executive is constitutionally empowered to conduct foreign policy and military operations unencumbered by the other two branches, at least when the rights of individuals are involved. With regard to Hamdi's challenge, the court concluded, "Plainly, the process Hamdi has received is not that to which he is entitled under the Due Process Clause" (542 US 538). It did leave open the option for the government to accord Hamdi due process within the military justice system by observing, "There remains the possibility that the standards we have articulated could be met by an appropriately authorized and properly constituted military tribunal." (542 US 538). The administration took the Supreme Court up on the option to create a tribunal within the military.

Subsequent to the Hamdi case, on November 12, 2001 President Bush issued a military order creating military tribunals to try any individual who was not a US citizen and who provided assistance to the 9/11 attacks. The military order followed the precedent established by President Franklin Roosevelt, who appointed a military tribunal in 1942 to try eight Germans who entered the United States by submarine. The Supreme Court had upheld the jurisdiction represented in that EO (Fisher, 2017, 252). In a brief for the circuit court, the government made an inherent presidential power argument tracing President Bush's authority to establish military tribunals to the establishment of the US Constitution, arguing, "it was well established when the Constitution was written and ratified that one of the powers inherent in military command was the authority to initiate tribunals for punishing enemy violations of the laws of war" (Brief for Appellants, cited in Fisher, 2017, 253, n. 17). Congress also provided a statute relating to detainees held in Cuba. The Detainee Treatment Act (DTA) of 2005 provided that "no court ... shall have jurisdiction to hear or consider ... an application for ... habeas corpus filed by ... an alien detained ... at Guantanamo Bay."

In 2001, Hamden, a Yemeni national, was captured in Afghanistan and turned over to US Armed Forces which transported him to Guantanamo Bay. A year later, President Bush deemed him eligible for trial by the military commission and he was charged with conspiring to commit offenses triable by the commission. In a habeas corpus petition to federal court, Hamden asserted that the military commission lacked the authority to try him, because no congressional Act nor the common laws of war supported trial by the commission for conspiracy, and the procedure adopted to try him violated basic tenets of military and international law. The claimed violation included the principle that a defendant must be permitted to see and hear the evidence against them, and he was not afforded that permission.

The government argued that the DTA repealed the courts' jurisdiction to review the decision, and that the Supreme Court should abstain under a previous precedent that, as a matter of comity, federal courts should normally abstain from intervening in pending courts-martial against service members. The court declared, "The assertion that military discipline and, therefore, the Armed Forces efficient operation are best served if the military justice system acts without regular interference from civilian courts is inapt, because Hamden is not a service member" (*Hamden* v. *Rumsfeld*, 126 S. Ct. 2749 [2006]). The court also stated: "The view that federal courts should respect the balance Congress struck when it created 'an integrated system of military courts and review procedures' is inapposite, since the tribunal convened to try Hamden is not part of the integrated system" (*Hamden* v. *Rumsfeld*, 548 US 557 ([2006]).

Further, the court declared:

(1) the military commission at issue is not expressly authorized by any congressional Act (548 US 567);

(2) neither the AUMF nor the DTA can be read to provide specific overriding authorization for the commission (548 US 594);

(3) the military commission at issue lacks the power to proceed because its structure and procedures violate both the Universal Code of Military Justice (UCMJ) and the four Geneva Conventions (548 US 625);

(4) there is a basis to presume that the procedures employed during Hamden's trial will violate the law, because UCMJ Article 36 has not been complied with (548 US 621);

(5) even assuming that Hamden is a dangerous individual who would cause great harm or death to innocent civilians given the opportunity, the executive must nevertheless comply with the prevailing rule of law in undertaking to try him and subject him to criminal punishment (548 US 635).

Two other cases involving the administration's response to terrorism and the military actions in Afghanistan focused on the legality of detaining foreign nationals at Guantanamo Bay and what legal rights they had under American law. One of the factors that the administration considered in detaining prisoners at Guantanamo was that it assumed it would be considered outside the jurisdiction of American courts. In a World War II case, *Johnson* v. *Eisentrager*, German citizens who had been captured by US forces in China had been tried and convicted of war crimes by an American military commission in Nanking and incarcerated in a prison in occupied Germany. In that case, the Supreme Court had concluded that the detainees had no right to the writ of habeas corpus, and thus, no access to American courts (*Johnson* v. *Eisentrager*, 70 S. Ct. 936 [1950]).

In the case of *Rasul* v. *Bush*, Rasul had been imprisoned at Guantanamo, and he contended in federal court that he was being held in federal custody in violation of US laws. The Supreme Court addressed the question whether US courts lack jurisdiction to consider challenges to the legality of the detention of foreign nationals captured abroad in connection with hostilities and incarcerated at Guantanamo.

The court had to consider whether the habeas statute which provides courts with authority to consider applications for habeas corpus confers a right to judicial review of the legality of executive detention of aliens in a territory over which the United States exercises plenary and exclusive jurisdiction, but not ultimate sovereignty (*Rasul* v. *Bush*, 542 US 466, 473 ([2009]).

The government argued that, through long-standing principles of American law, congressional legislation is presumed not to have extraterritorial application unless such intent is clearly manifested. The court disagreed and maintained that whatever traction the presumption against territoriality might have in other contexts, it certainly had no application to the operation of the habeas statute with respect to persons detained within the territorial jurisdiction of the United States and, by the express terms of its agreements with Cuba, the United States exercised complete jurisdiction and control over Guantanamo Bay (542 US 479). Further, the court reasoned, there was little reason to think that Congress intended the geographical coverage of the statute to vary depending on the detainee's citizenship. (542 US 479).

The government had argued that the precedent in the case of *Johnson* v. *Eisentrager* applied to this case and barred federal court jurisdiction.

The court disagreed and stated that the petitioners detained at Guantanamo differed from those in the previous case, in that they were not nationals at war with the United States, they denied having engaged in acts of aggression, and they had never been afforded access to any tribunal, much less charged and convicted of wrongdoing (542 US 475). Thus, the court clearly indicated that due process rights and access to American courts would trump claims of the authority of the executive, even in this area of defense policy and management.

Another case involving detainees in the battle against terrorists also focused on detainees' access to courts. In response to the Supreme Court's decision in *Hamden* v. *Rumsfeld*, Congress passed the Military Commission Act (MCA) (10 USC sec. 948a et. seq. [2006]) which amended the DTA. It provides that, "No court, justice, or judge shall have jurisdiction to hear or consider an application for a writ of habeas corpus filed by or on behalf of an alien detained by the United States who has been determined by the United States to have been properly detained as an enemy combatant or is awaiting such determination." After the Supreme Court's decision in the Hamdi case, the deputy secretary of defense established Combatant Status Review Panels (CSRTs) to determine whether "enemy combatants detained at Guantanamo were enemy combatants," as the Department of Defense defined that term. A later memorandum established the procedures to implement the CSRTs.

Several foreign nationals were detained by the Department of Defense pursuant to the AUMF and each was determined to be an enemy combatant. Each filed for a writ of habeas corpus. The Court of Appeals for the District of Columbia Circuit ruled that the MCA properly stripped federal courts from all jurisdiction over the detainees. Two months later, after initially declining the appeal, a majority of the Supreme Court announced that it had taken the unusual step of reconsidering the appeals.

In *Boumediene* v. *Bush* (553 US 723 [2008]), the question the Supreme Court addressed was whether the MCA denies the federal courts jurisdiction to hear habeas corpus actions pending at the time of its enactment. The detainees argued that the MCA was not a sufficiently clear statute to strip the federal courts of jurisdiction, and that they had cognizable rights that were violated by the terms of the statute. The government contended that noncitizens designated as enemy combatants and detained in territory located outside the nation's borders have no constitutional rights and no privilege of habeas corpus. The court reviewed the right to seek the writ of habeas corpus dating back to the nation's founding. It concluded that the Framers deemed the writ to be an essential mechanism in the separation of powers and protection of rights of the detained by a means consistent with the essential design of the US Constitution (553 US 743). The court also concluded that the detainees were held in a territory that, while not technically part of the United States, was under the complete control of the US government; thus, habeas corpus had full effect at Guantanamo (553 US 770).

The Supreme Court found deficiencies in the processes the government was using, including the absence of a release remedy and specific language allowing AUMF challenges (553 US 787). The court held that the procedures for review of detainees' status provided in the DTA were not an adequate and effective substitute for habeas corpus (553 US 723). However, those were not the only problems that the court identified. In fact, even if the government changed the processes to remedy those problems, the court insisted that the detainees must still have available the opportunity to present evidence to a court if they could present reasonably available evidence demonstrating there was no basis for their detention (553 US 789). The court emphasized that as far as the separation of powers was concerned, it viewed judicial redress to be crucial to the balance of powers (553 US 796). It held that detainees may invoke the fundamental procedural protections of habeas corpus (553 US 796). In doing so, the court emphasized that it saw habeas corpus as a fundamental constitutional issue (553 US 796).

Thus, in declaring its position with respect to the separation of powers issue, the court made it clear that it would be the arbiter of where the balance should lie. Even if the executive acted pursuant to a statute passed by Congress, the court would show no reticence in invalidating the executive action if it appeared to contravene what it understood as a central right guaranteed by the US Constitution. "Their message was clear, a majority was not going to relinquish judicial authority to hear all challenges from detainees, even those at a base that the federal government had wanted to be beyond such jurisdiction" (Biskupic, 2009, 342).

These detainee cases carried more significance than just their impact on restructuring the procedures for holding detainees. Walter Dellinger, a former US solicitor general, declared that the Hamden case ranked with the Supreme Court's decisions in the Truman steel seizure case and the Nixon tape-recordings case in terms of the court limiting executive power. He stated

> a short while back, there seemed to be no stopping the sweeping and untenable assertions of a presidential power to disregard laws that seemed entirely constitutional to me. I had thought we had effectively lost the principle that the president – indeed the whole executive branch of government – was really required to comply with valid federal laws constitutionally enacted by Congress. Now I think that principle has been not merely affirmed but also re-enshrined. How many cases can be more important than that? (Dellinger, 2006, 2).

Dellinger explained that the meaning of the decision goes to the core of the question of the president being bound by law:

> It's about all those laws the president says, as he signs them, that he will not commit to obey, if in his view foreign relations or deliberative processes of the executive or other matters may be affected. And, by the way, he won't even commit to tell Congress he is not obeying the law. That is what this is about. (Dellinger, 2006, 3)

Like President Clinton, President Bush also tried to regulate labor relations by EO and was similarly unsuccessful. In *Building and Construction Trades Department* v. *Albaugh*, a district court considered a broad constitutional claim by the president that the US Constitution's Take Care Clause allowed him to regulate labor relations involving federal contracts.

In 2001, George W. Bush issued EO 13202 prohibiting federal agencies or recipients of federal funding from requiring or prohibiting Project Labor Agreements (PLAs) – "prehire" collective bargaining agreements – in bid specifications for construction contracts. Plaintiffs cited a number of projects that both anticipated receipt of federal funding and expressed an intention to utilize a PLA. The government's argument for the order's legal basis was that it rested on the "well-established" power of the president to take care that laws are faithfully executed, and this justified an action without any other basis in the Constitution or in statutes. As such, it was an "inherent power" argument. The district court observed that in *Youngstown Sheet & Tube Co.* v. *Sawyer* in the Truman administration (see Section 2), the government had argued that the general Article II power of the president to take care that the laws are faithfully executed justified an action without any other basis in the Constitution or in statutes, and the Supreme Court had rejected that argument. The court in this case declared: "In the framework of our Constitution, the President's power to see that the laws are faithfully executed refutes the idea that he is to be a lawmaker" (*Bldg. Constr. Trades Dept.* v. *Allbaugh*, 172 F Supp. 2d 159 [2001]).

The district court then went on to consider whether or not the EO was preempted by the NLRA. It held that it was, and declared: "In the guise of preserving open competition and government neutrality, EO 13202 has altered the balance of power between labor unions and employers on federally funded construction projects" (172 F. Supp. 2d 161). The court cited the Supreme Court's action in the Clinton administration case, *Chamber of Commerce* v. *Reich*, which had held that the NLRA preempts the president from interfering with the labor market through an EO. It found that because the NLRA specific-ally authorizes the use of PLAs by private employers, EO 13202's prohibition of required PLAs did violate the Act. The court declared: "Private entities are being prohibited by EO13202 from requiring PLAs that are expressly allowed by the NLRA" (172 F. Supp. 2d 167). It concluded that the president had exceeded his constitutional and statutory authority. Accordingly, enforcement of EO 13202 was permanently enjoined by the court. The president had thus tried to alter federal relations policy by EO and was turned down by the courts which made it clear that such alterations could only be achieved by congressional action.

Barack Obama (2009–2017)

A case that bridged the Bush and Obama administrations involved the power of the president to recognize foreign governments on behalf of the nation. In its decision, the Supreme Court pared back the use of the "sole organ doctrine" stated in the Curtiss-Wright decision (discussed in Section 2) that had been asserted by the executive branch for decades. The case involved Israel's claim that Jerusalem was its official capital. No president had issued an official statement acknowledging any country's sovereignty over Jerusalem, and the executive had constantly maintained that the status of Jerusalem should not be decided unilaterally but in consultation with all concerned. The State Department's Foreign Affairs Manual (FAM) does not allow citizens to list a sovereign that conflicts with executive branch policy.

Congress passed the Foreign Relations Authorization Act, Fiscal Year 2003 and section 214 sought to override the FAM by allowing citizens born in Jerusalem to list their place of birth as "Israel." When George W. Bush signed the Act, he issued a signing statement that US policy regarding Jerusalem had not changed. Ziyotofsky was a man born to US citizens living in Jerusalem, and his mother requested a passport and consular report of birth abroad for him; she asked that his place of birth be listed as Jerusalem, Israel. The embassy clerks explained that pursuant to State Department policy, the passport would only list Jerusalem. The parents brought suit under section 214 and claimed that he had a right to have Israel as his place of birth on his passport.

The secretary of state contended that in accordance with the Curtiss-Wright case, the president has "exclusive authority to conduct diplomatic relations," and quoted the Curtiss-Wright statement which described the president as "the sole organ" of the federal government in the field of international relations. The Supreme Court declared that it "declines to acknowledge that unbounded power" and, further, that "The Curtiss-Wright case does not extend so far as the Secretary suggests." Moreover, the court explained, "Curtiss-Wright did not hold that the President is free from Congress's lawmaking power in the field of international relations" (*Zivotofsky* v. *Kerry*, 576 US 1 ([2015])).

Notwithstanding its general declarations concerning that the president's power in foreign relations is not unlimited, the Supreme Court in this case did uphold the president's right to recognize foreign countries and declared that power resides in the president alone. The court stated that while that power extends no further than the formal recognition determination, Congress may not enact a law that directly contradicts it. It found that section 214 amounted to an improper act for Congress to "aggrandize its power at the expense of another branch" by requiring the President to contradict an earlier recognition determination in an official document issued by the executive branch "To allow Congress to control the President's communication in the context of a formal recognition determination is to allow Congress to exercise that exclusive power itself. As a result, the statute is unconstitutional" (576 US 36).

President Obama attempted to change immigration policy by EO. He gave a speech on November 20, 2014 announcing an immigration policy that would apply to four million undocumented aliens who had a son or daughter who was a US citizen or lawful permanent resident. This was called the Deferred Action for Parents of Americans and Lawful Permanent Residents Program (DAPA). The program set forth how federal prosecutors should exercise prosecutorial discretion before enforcing immigration law. Among the benefits accruing to persons subject to the program were eligibility for relevant social security disability benefits, eligibility for Medicare Part A health insurance, earned income tax credits, and eligibility for state driver's licenses and unemployment benefits. Of the approximately 11. 3 million illegal aliens in the US, 4.3 million would have been eligible for DAPA. In *Texas* v. *United States*, Texas and twenty-five other states challenged the secretary of homeland security's order establishing the program. The district court concluded that Texas had shown a considerable probability that the program violated the APA, and it issued a preliminary injunction barring implementation (*Texas* v. *United States*, 809 F 3d 134 ([2015]). The federal government challenged the states' standing to sue, but the district court and the Fifth Circuit Court concluded that the states did have standing, because DAPA would require them to issue driver's licenses and the costs of doing so constituted a cognizable injury.

The government argued that its order was procedural and did not require notice and comment rulemaking under the APA. The First Circuit Court disagreed and concluded, "An agency rule that modifies substantive rights and interests can only be nominally procedural, and the exemption for such rules of agency procedure cannot apply. DAPA modifies substantive rights and interests – conferring lawful presence on 500,000 illegal aliens in Texas forcing the state to choose between spending millions of dollars to subsidize driver's licenses and changing its law" (*Texas* v. *United States*, 787 F 3d 733, 766 ([2015]). In a *per curium* opinion the Supreme Court approved the judgment of the circuit court without additional written findings or rationale.

President Obama, like Presidents Clinton and George W. Bush before him, faced pushback from the courts in the labor relations area. On January 4, 2012, in a case involving presidential appointments to the National Labor Relations Board (NLRB), President Obama attempted to appoint three new members to the board pursuant to Article II, section 2, clause 3 – the Recess Appointments Clause of the US Constitution. At that time, the Senate was operating pursuant to a unanimous consent agreement, which provided that the Senate would meet in pro forma session every three business days from December 20, 2011, through January 23, 2012, and the agreement stated that there would be no business conducted during those sessions. However, on December 23, the Senate overrode its prior agreement by unanimous consent and passed a temporary extension of the payroll tax. During the January 3 pro forma session, the Senate acted to convene the second session of the 112th Congress and to fulfill its constitutional duty to meet on January 3.

Noel Canning petitioned a federal court for review of the NLRB's decision that Obama had violated the NLRA. He maintained that the decision of the board was not valid because three of the members were appointed under the aegis of putative recess appointments when the Senate was not in recess, and the vacancies which the three appointees were to fill did not happen during the recess of the Senate as required for recess appointments by the Constitution. Canning argued that "the Recess" in the Appointments Clause refers to the intersession recess between sessions of the Senate when the Senate, by definition, is not in session and therefore unavailable to receive nominations from the president. The NLRB argued that the appointment procedure is available during the intrasession "recesses" or breaks in the Senate's business when it is otherwise in a continuing session.

The US Court of Appeals for the District of Columbia Circuit observed,

> An interpretation of "the Recess" that permits the President to decide when the Senate is in recess would demolish the checks and balances inherent in the advice-and-consent requirement, giving the President free rein to appoint his desired nominees at any time he pleases, whether that time be a weekend, lunch, or even when the Senate is in session, and he is merely displeased with its inaction. This cannot be the law. (*Noel Canning* v. *NLRB*, 705 F 3d 490, 503 ([2012])

The court held that "the Recess" is limited to intersession recesses, and the president made his three appointments after Congress began a new session and while that session continued. As a result, the court held that the appointments were invalid (705 F 3d 505). It further held that the board vacancies did not arise during the intersession recess of the Senate (705 F 3d 512). Accordingly, the court concluded that because none of the three appointments were valid, the board lacked a quorum, and its decision involving Canning must be vacated.

5 Presidents Donald Trump and Joe Biden

Donald Trump (2017–2021)

One of Donald Trump's primary campaign promises was to tighten up US immigration policy and management. To try to fulfill the promise, he issued EO 13768 aimed at cities that had proclaimed themselves sanctuary cities. The EO was framed in order to prevent such cities from limiting their cooperation with federal agencies dealing with illegal immigrants. The order directed the attorney general to ensure that local governments which did not supply information to federal immigration authorities would be ineligible to receive federal grants. Cities suing to stop implementation of the order took one of two approaches: either (1) against Trump and his appointees, and the EO itself; or (2) against the attorney general for his actions in attempting to implement the EO.

With respect to the first approach, the City of Santa Clara and the City and County of San Francisco sued Trump, the attorney general, the secretary of homeland security, and the director of the OMB, challenging the constitutionality of the EO as violating the separation of powers doctrine by depriving them of their Tenth and Fifth Amendment rights, and of hundreds of millions of dollars of federal grants that supported core services.

In *Santa Clara* v. *Trump,* the district court concluded:

(1) The EO's attempt to place new conditions on federal funds was an improper endeavor to wield Congress's exclusive spending power and a violation of the Constitution's separation of powers principles (*Cnty. of Santa Clara v. Trump* 250 F Supp. 3d 497, 531 [2017]).

(2) The EO violated the Spending Clause (of the US Constitution), because conditions placed on congressional spending must have some nexus with the purpose of the implicated funds, and the order expressly targeted defunding grants that had no nexus to immigration enforcement at all (250 F Supp. 3d 533).

(3) By denying sanctuary jurisdictions, all federal grants, hundreds of millions of dollars on which the Counties relied, the threat was unconstitutionally coercive (250 F Supp. 3d 533).

(4) The order's threat to pull all federal grants from jurisdictions that refused to honor detainer requests or to bring enforcement action against them violated the Tenth Amendment's prohibitions against commandeering (250 F Supp. 3d 534). As a result, the district court issued a nationwide injunction against officials (other than Trump) from enforcing the law against jurisdictions they deemed as constituting sanctuary cities.

With regard to the second approach, four federal courts issued opinions addressing determinations by the attorney general to withhold funding under specific federal programs from particular jurisdictions, because they were sanctuary jurisdictions. One example was *City of Chicago* v. *Sessions* (888 F 3d 272 [2018]). The City of Chicago sued the attorney general for enforcement of two conditions imposed upon it as a recipient of the Edward Byrne Memorial Justice Assistance Grant (JAG) Program. The attorney general tied receipt of the funds to the grant recipient's compliance with these conditions, which the city argued were unlawful and unconstitutional: (1) a mandate of advance notice to federal authorities of the release date of persons in state or local custody who were believed to be aliens, and (2) a requirement that the local correctional facility should ensure federal agents access to such facilities and meet with those persons.

The circuit court found that none of the Byrne law's provisions granted the attorney general the authority to impose conditions that required state or local governments to assist in immigration enforcement, nor to deny funds to states or governments for failure to comply with those conditions (888 F 3d 283). The court concluded that the Byrne JAG statute provides the attorney general with authority over a carefully delineated list of actions, with no such broad authority to impose other conditions he finds reasonable. The court opined, "If Congress had wanted to vest such authority in the Attorney General – regarding the Byrne JAG grant – one would expect it to include explicit language in the grant statute itself, as it did in the Violence Against Women Act" (888 F 3d 286).

The court explicitly spoke to the separation of powers issue,

> The power of the purse does not belong to the Executive Branch. It rests in the Legislative Branch. Congress, may of course, delegate such authority to the Executive Branch, and indeed the case today turns on whether it did so here, but the Executive Branch does not otherwise have the inherent authority as to the grant at issue here to condition the payment of such federal funds on adherence to its political priorities. (888 F 3d 283)

The circuit court thus found no congressional grant of authority to the executive and denied any inherent executive authority to change the terms of the JAG program.

President Trump also tried to limit travel into the United States from certain countries in response to the COVID-19 crisis, by acting to restrict travel by residents of these countries. His first attempts were rejected by the federal courts. His first travel ban order, EO 13769, suspended the US Refugee Admissions Program for 120 days, lowered the number of refugees that could be admitted to 50,000, suspended the entry of Syrian refugees indefinitely, suspended entry of aliens from seven countries (Iran, Iraq, Somalia, Sudan, Libya, Syria and Yemen) for 90 days until better vetting procedures could be developed, provided an exemption for religious minorities in the listed countries, and allowed for some exemptions on a case-by-case basis.

The states of Washington and Minnesota sued the President and asked the federal court to enjoin its implementation. A federal district court in Seattle issued an injunction on the first travel ban order on the grounds that, among other things, it violated the US Constitution's Due Process Clause because it was not clear who exactly the travel ban applied to.

In *Washington v. Trump* (847 F 3d 1151 [9th Cir. 2017]), the Ninth Circuit Court of Appeals considered the government's appeal of the district court's restraining order. The government argued that the district court lacked subject matter jurisdiction because the states have no standing to sue. The circuit court disagreed, and agreed with the states that had argued that the teaching and research missions of their universities would be harmed by the EO's effects on their faculty and students who could not travel for research, academic collaboration, or for personal reasons, and on their families abroad who could not visit. The court found that the interests of the states were aligned with their students and, as administators of state universities, the states could assert not only their own rights to the extent affected by the EO but may also the rights of their students and faculty members (847 F 3d 1160).

The government's brief also argued that the district court lacked authority to enjoin enforcement of the EO because, it was asserted, the president has unreviewable authority to suspend the admission of any class of aliens and that the president's decisions about immigration policy, particularly when motivated by national security concerns, are unreviewable – even if those actions potentially contravene constitutional rights and protections. In essence, this was an inherent authority argument based on the president's status as commander in chief as well as the separation of powers. The circuit court strongly rejected that argument and declared,

> Although our jurisprudence has long counseled deference to the political branches on matters of immigration and national security, neither the Supreme Court or our court has ever held that courts lack the authority to

review executive action in those arenas for compliance with the Constitution. To the contrary, the Supreme Court has repeatedly and explicitly rejected the notion that the political branches have unreviewable authority over immigration or are not subject to the Constitution when policymaking in that context. (847 F 3d 1161).

The court referenced the Supreme Court's decision in the *Boumediene* case (discussed in Section 4), observing: "Indeed, federal courts routinely review the constitutionality of – and even invalidate – actions taken by the executive to promote national security, and have done so, even in times of conflict" (847 F 3d 1163). The court also referenced the Hamdi case (discussed in Section 4) and declared, "Whatever power the United States Constitution envisions for the Executive in its exchanges with other nations or with enemy organizations in times of conflict, it most assuredly envisions a role for all three branches when individual liberties are at stake" (1163).

The states argued that the EO violated the procedural due process rights of various aliens. However, the government argued that most or all of the individuals affected by the EO had no rights under the Due Process Clause. The court rejected that argument.

The circuit court concluded that the government had failed to establish that it would likely succeed on its due process argument in the appeal and refused to lift the restraining order prohibiting implementation of the EO (847 F 3d 1167–1168). The administration informed the court that it would replace the first order with a new one.

The new ban, invoked by EO 13780, dropped Iraq from the list of countries, no longer applied to green card holders or people with valid visas inside the United States, lifted the permanent ban on Syrian refugees, and removed the exemption for minorities. The district court in Hawaii issued a temporary restraining order in *Hawaii* v. *Trump* (245 F Supp. 3d 1227 [D. Haw. 2017]). The court concluded that the plaintiffs stood a good chance of succeeding on First Amendment Establishment grounds, finding the order based on anti-Muslim sentiment. The court also concluded that there was questionable evidence to support the order on national security grounds. The Ninth Circuit Court of Appeals considered the government's appeal of the restraining order.

As in the previous case, the government argued that the State of Hawaii lacked standing to bring the suit under the Immigration and Nationality Act (INA) 1965. The Ninth Circuit Court disagreed. Similar to the previous case, the court found that the state's efforts to enroll students and hire faculty members who were nationals of the six designated countries fell within the zone of interests of the INA. Further, the court argued that the state's interest in effectuating its refugee resettlement policies and programs also fell withing the zone of interests protected by the INA. As it had argued in the previous case, the government contended that the court could not review the EO because the consular nonreviewability doctrine counsels that the decision to withhold a visa is not subject to judicial review. The court disagreed stating that the plaintiffs did not seek review of an individual consular officer's decision to grant or deny a visa. The case was justiciable, the court found, because the plaintiffs seeking judicial review of the EO were contending that it exceeds the statutory authority delegated by Congress and constitutional boundaries. The court opined: "Whatever deference we accord to the President's immigration and national security policy judgements does not preclude us from reviewing the policy at all" (*Hawaii* v. *Trump* 859 F 3d 741, 768 ([2017]).

On the merits of the case, the court observed that the law did give the president broad authority to suspend the entry of aliens or classes of aliens; it stated that this authority is not unbounded (859 F 3d 769). The court found, however, that Section 1182f of the INA

> requires the President *find* that the entry of a class of aliens into the United States *would be detrimental* to the interests of the United States. This section requires that the President's findings support the conclusion that entry of all nationals from the six designated countries, all refugees, and refugees in excess of 50,000 would be harmful to the national interest. There is no sufficient finding in EO2 that the entry of the excluded classes would be detrimental to the interests of the United States. (859 F 3d 769)

The court concluded that the EO did not offer a sufficient justification to suspend the entry of more than 180 million people on the basis of nationality: "National security is not a 'talismanic incantation' that, once invoked, can support any and all exercise of executive power under Section 1182f" (859 F 3d 773, no. 9). The court insisted that the president make a finding and support it; it was not accepting that the president could just proclaim "national security" and his inherent powers to protect it as a justification for his order. The court was, however, prepared to review and assess the underlying reasons and evidence for the claim that national security was threatened. The district court in Maryland reached a similar conclusion on the EO. The Fourth Circuit affirmed the order on Establishment Clause grounds.

On September 24, 2017, President Trump issued a new presidential proclamation limiting immigration from eight specified countries. The new proclamation seemed to be an attempt to address some of the circuit court's criticisms that the previous order had not provided sufficient determination of a detriment to the United States and sufficient support for such a conclusion.

In *Hawaii* v. *Trump*, the State of Hawaii and some private parties challenged President Trump's Proclamation no. 7645 that placed entry restrictions on the nationals of the eight foreign states whose systems for managing and sharing information about their nationals the president deemed inadequate based on a Department of Homeland Security review. The plaintiffs alleged the proclamation violated the INA and the Constitution's Establishment Clause.

This version of the travel ban was enjoined by a federal district court on October 17, 2017. The judge stated that the president exceeded his authority within the INA, and that the president did not meet the essential precondition to exercise his delegated authority, in that he must make a sufficient finding that the entry of these classes of people would be "detrimental to the interests of the United States." He also concluded that the president's actions run afoul of other provisions of the Act that protect against nationalities-based discrimination (859 F 3d 741).

On appeal, in *Trump* v. *Hawaii* (1385 S. Ct. 2392 [2018]), the Supreme Court reversed the lower court's decision. With regard to the INA, the court concluded, "By its plain language section 1182(f) grants the President broad discretion based on his findings – following a worldwide, multi-agency review – that entry of the covered aliens would be detrimental to the national interest" (1385 S. Ct. 2408). The plaintiffs had charged, in their Establishment Clause claim, that the proclamation exhibited religious bias by excluding Muslims. The Suprem Court disagreed and found in favor of the government concluding that "because there is persuasive evidence that the entry suspension has a legitimate grounding in national security concerns, quite apart from any religious hostility, we must accept that independent justification" (1385 S. Ct. 2421). Here, the court placed significant emphasis on its finding that the twelve-page proclamation – which thoroughly described the process, agency evaluations, and recommendations underlying the president's chosen restrictions – was more detailed than any prior order a president had issued under the statute. The court went on to observe that when the president adopts a preventative measure in the context of international affairs, he is not required to conclusively link all of the pieces of the puzzle before the courts grant weight to his empirical conclusions.

It is apparent that President Trump's attempts to impose travel restrictions on countries he perceived as a threat were significantly circumscribed by means of the federal judiciary's findings on the first two travel bans, and this led the administration to conduct a much more through and documented process for promulgating its ultimately successful travel ban. It cannot, however, be concluded that the federal courts gave the president free rein to impose any travel restrictions he chose, based on the statute and his authority as commander in chief. This was quite different from the treatment President Roosevelt's EO received for sequestering Japanese Americans.

The Trump administration did prevail on another border issue involving the reprogramming of Defense Department funds. In his 2018 budget proposal, President Trump requested $5.8 billion for construction of a wall across the US southwestern border pursuant to his campaign promise to construct a border wall. The House of Representatives refused the request and the final appropriation did not include the funding. Trump issued a proclamation (no. 9844) under the National Emergencies Act (50 USC sec. 1601–1651) declaring that a national emergency existed at the southern border. It described "a border security and humanitarian crisis that threatens core national security interests," because the border served as a major entry point for criminals, gang members, and illicit narcotics and the number of family units entering the United States had recently increased. It declared the emergency situation necessitated support from the armed forces, and it made construction authority available to the Department of Defense.

Trump ordered the Defense Department to transfer $2.5 billion to pay for border wall projects, with new barriers extending up to 130 miles within Arizona, California, and New Mexico. The secretary of defense relied upon section 8005 of the Department of Defense Appropriations Act of 2019 to reprogram the money, moving funds from the Defense Department to the Department of Homeland Security. Section 8005 authorized the secretary of defense to transfer funds for military purposes if the secretary determined that the transfer was "for high priority items based on unforeseen military requirements" and "the item for which funds are requested have not been denied by Congress" (Public Law No. 115–245, sec. 8005).

The Sierra Club and the Southern Border Communities Coalition filed suit against President Trump, Defense Secretary Shanahan, Homeland Security Secretary Nielsen, and Treasury Secretary Mnuchin. They alleged that the officials exceeded the scope of their constitutional and statutory authority by spending money in excess of what Congress allocated for border security; that the officials' actions violated separation of powers principles as well as the Appropriations Clause and the Presentment Clause of the Constitution; and that the officials failed to comply with the National Environmental Policy Act. They also alleged that the officials were acting ultra vires in seeking to divert funding without statutory authority to do so. The district court held that the plaintiffs were entitled to a preliminary injunction with respect to the section 8005 reprogramming authority, because they would likely succeed in arguing that the officials had acted ultra vires, that they had been irreparably harmed, and that the balance of equities weighed in their favor.

On appeal, the Ninth Circuit Court of Appeals decided the appeal from the district court's imposition of a preliminary injunction against the reprogramming of the funds in a 2:1 ruling. The majority considered the basis for the plaintiffs constitutional and statutory claims and observed that the Sierra Club claimed that to the extent that the officials did not have statutory authority to reprogram the funds, the officials acted in violation of constitutional separation of powers principles, because they lacked any background constitutional authority to appropriate funds – making the Sierra Club's claim fundamentally a constitutional one. The majority stated that the Sierra Club could bring their challenge through an equitable action to enjoin unconstitutional official conduct, or under the judicial review procedures of the APA (*Sierra Club* v. *Trump* 929 F 3d 670, 694 ([2019]).

The majority found with respect to the requirement of section 8005 that the need for the funding must be unforeseen, the long history of the president's efforts to build a border barrier, and of Congress's refusal to appropriate the funds he requested, made it implausible that the need was unforeseen.

The dissenting judge did not agree with the majority's finding that the Sierra Club's claim in alleging a constitutional violation was legitimate. Instead, the dissenting judge stated that the proper approach was to consider the challenge in terms of an alleged statutory violation. As such, the judge concluded that the Sierra Club had neither an implied statutory cause of action under section 8005 nor an equitable cause of action to challenge the reprogramming under the APA, as they fall outside the zone of interests for such a claim. Accordingly, the judge concluded that the government had made a strong showing that it was likely to succeed on the merits of its appeal (929 F 3d 709).

The Supreme Court seemed to agree with the Ninth Circuit dissenting judge. In a short *per curium* opinion for which little explanation wasw provided, the court, with only one justice concurring in part and dissenting in part, stayed the lower court's injunction, which allowed the reprogramming to go forward while a fuller hearing on the merits of the suit proceeded. The only explanation the court provided was: "Among the reasons is that the Government has made a sufficient showing at this stage that the plaintiffs have no cause of action to obtain review of the Acting Secretary's compliance with section 8005" (*Trump* v. *Sierra Club* 150, S. Ct. 1 ([2019]).

The Supreme Court clearly did not endorse the Court of Appeals panel's constitutional reasoning and treated the case as one of statutory interpretation. The government argued (as had the dissenting judge) that the plaintiffs were not proper plaintiffs under a straightforward application of the zone of interests requirement for a legitimate cause of action to bring the suit.

President Trump also attempted to implement his immigration policy by reversing one of his predecessor's key programs. The Trump administration tried to repeal President Obama's initiative to allow noncitizens who entered the United States as children to remain in the country and not face deportation. That move was challenged in federal court and was decided by the Supreme Court. In *Regents of the University of California* v. *United States Department of Homeland Security* (908, F 3d 476 [2018]), twenty-six states challenged the secretary's decision to repeal the previous secretary's decision that established the Deferred Action for Childhood Arrivals program (DACA), which allows those noncitizens who entered the United States as children to apply for two-year renewable periods of deferred action from deportation. The secretary, on the legal advice of the attorney general, found that DACA was illegal from its inception and therefore could no longer continue in effect.

The government contended that the secretary's decision was unreviewable and outside the court's jurisdiction, because the decision was pursuant to the Department of Homeland Security's discretion to enforce or not enforce deportation under the Immigration and Nationality Act. A Supreme Court majority disagreed and found that the decision was justified under the APA. The court observed that the Department of Homeland Security could rescind DACA, but that it had to follow the APA in doing so (*Department of Homeland Security* v. *Regents of the University of California*, 140 S. Ct. 1891, 1914 ([2020]). It found that the Department of Homeland Security had not provided adequate reasons for the recission, in that the secretary had failed to assess whether DACA recipients had relied upon the previous secretary's memorandum and what the consequences were for them (140 S. Ct. 1891). The court recognized the executive's basic authority to make the decision but insisted it follow required procedure.

Joe Biden (2021–)

President Biden was a most active issuer of executive directives right from the start of his administration. He issued 29 directives within 3 days of taking office and, after 100 days, he had issued more than 100 EOs, proclamations, memoranda, and other executive actions. As of April 29, 2021, his first year in office, he had issued thirty-one EOs, more than twice the number issued by either Obama (nineteen) or Bush (eleven), and two-thirds more than Trump (twenty-five) (New Civil Liberties Alliance, 2021).

On September 9, 2021, President Biden announced a comprehensive plan to mandate COVID-19 vaccines nationwide. Pursuant to his plan, he issued two

EOs: one mandating vaccines for federal workers (EO 14043) and one for federal contractors (EO 14042). He also asked the Department of Labor to issue an emergency rule compelling all employers with 100 or more employees to require their workers to be vaccinated or for any unvaccinated workers to produce a negative COVID-19 test at least once a week. The requirement carried a $14,000 fine per violation and would have affected two-thirds of the country's workforce. Biden also announced that the Department of Health and Human Services would require employees in health-care facilities that receive Medicare or Medicaid reimbursement to be vaccinated – a requirement, Biden said, that would impact seven million workers at 50,000 health-care providers (The White House, 2021). He also ordered the Department of Defense to look into imposing a vaccine order.

All four presidential mandates were challenged in federal court. To implement the vaccine requirement for employees, the secretary of labor issued an emergency standard (86 Fed. Reg. 61402 [2021]) pursuant to the Occupational Safety and Health Act (84 Stat. 1590, 29 USC sec. 651) that embodied the president's mandate for all employers with 100 or more workers. The order was challenged by the State of Ohio, and other states, and the National Federation of Independent Business. The Supreme Court issued its opinion and an order staying the implementation of the emergency standard. In addressing the question whether the statute plainly authorized the mandate, the court stated that it did not. It stated that it expected Congress to speak clearly when authorizing an agency to exercise powers of vast economic and political significance. The court declared that "Administrative agencies are creatures of statute. They accordingly possess only the authorities that Congress has provided." It further stated: "the Act empowers the Secretary to set *workplace* safety standards, not broad public health measures" (*National Federation of Independent Business* v. *OSHA*, 595 US___2022, 6).

The court observed that, "Permitting OSHA to regulate the hazards of daily life – simply because most Americans have jobs and face the same risks while on the clock – would significantly expand OSHA's regulatory authority without clear congressional approval" (595 US___2022, 7). It concluded: "OSHA's indiscriminate approach fails to account for this crucial distinction – between occupational risk and risk more generally – and accordingly the mandate takes on the character of a general public health measure, rather than an '*occupational* safety or health standard'" (595 US___2022, 7). Thus, the court clearly rejected the administration's more expansive interpretation of the statute.

A second COVID-19 related case involved a vaccine mandate for health workers. Pursuant to Biden's announcement on November 5, 2021, the secretary of health and human services issued an interim rule amending the existing conditions of participation in Medicare and Medicaid to add a new requirement that facilities ensure that their covered staff are vaccinated against COVID-19. Two states, Missouri and Louisiana, filed suits challenging the rule and two district courts found the rule defective and entered preliminary injunctions against it.

The government's appeals to the circuit courts were denied and the Supreme Court accepted an appeal to review the district court's decisions. In interpreting the statute governing the two health programs (Rules and Regulations: Impact Analyses of Medicare and Medicaid Rules and Regulations on Hospitals, 42 USC sec.1302[a]), the Eastern District of Missouri District Court concluded that given the nature and breadth of the vaccine mandate, it required clear authorization from Congress, and Congress had not provided it (*Biden* v. *Missouri*, 571 F Supp. 3d 1079 [2021]).

The Supreme Court disagreed with the district court and stated that Congress had authorized the secretary's action in the statute to impose conditions on the receipt of Medicare and Medicaid funds that the secretary finds necessary in the interests of the health and safety of individuals that are furnished with services (*Biden* v. *Missouri*, 142 S. Ct. 647 [2022] 652). The court observed that hospitals had long been required under the department's regulations to implement programs to govern the surveillance, prevention, and control of infectious diseases and that health-care workers are ordinarily required to be vaccinated for various diseases (142 S. Ct. 653).

For another vaccine mandate, President Biden directed the Department of Defense to look into how and when the department would add COVID-19 vaccination to the list of required vaccinations for members of the military. Thereafter, the department and the Navy issued a series of orders implementing the requirement for COVID-19 vaccination. The commander of the Navy Special Warfare Service issued Trident Order #12 which set a deadline of October 17, 2021 for unvaccinated service members to receive their first jab or submit exception requests. It provided that exemptions for medical and administrative (including religious) reasons would be adjudicated via service policies, and special operations personnel who refused to receive the vaccine based solely on personal or religious beliefs would still be medically disqualified.

Thirty-five Navy Special Warfare Service members filed suit alleging that the military's mandatory vaccination policy violated their religious freedom under the First Amendment and the Religious Freedom Restoration Act (RFRA). They requested a preliminary injunction to prevent the order from being implemented. The federal district court observed that courts generally refrained from reviewing military orders. It will be recalled that the Supreme Court in the

Japanese exclusion case declined to review the military commander's judgment. However, since then, federal courts have decided that some military
issues are appropriate for judicial review, and they have devised tests for
deciding the appropriateness of such reviews.

Applying these, the district court declared: "The Navy provides
a religious accommodation process, but by all accounts, it is theatre"
(*United States Navy Seals 1–26* v. *Biden*, 578 F Supp. 3d 822, 826 [2022]).
The court found: that the specific violations of rights under the First
Amendment and the RFRA constituted strong claims; that loss of First
Amendment freedoms constitute irreparable injury; that whether denying
religious accommodation violates the First Amendment is a distinct legal
question which would not seriously impede the military in the performance
of its vital duties; and that whether the vaccine mandate passes muster under
the First Amendment and the RFRA requires neither military expertise or
discretion. Thus, the court concluded that all these factors favored granting
court jurisdiction (578 F Supp. 3d 833–835).

Both the district court and the circuit court found that under the RFRA the
Navy had not demonstrated a compelling interest which required more than just
claiming broad national security interests. The circuit court found that multiple
plaintiffs were successfully deployed overseas after the vaccine became available. The circuit court agreed with the district court that the Navy had not shown
a compelling interest to deny religious accommodation to the plaintiffs (*U.S.
Navy Seals* v. *Biden* 27 F 4th 336 ([2022]). The circuit court concluded that the
plaintiffs' First Amendment freedoms were seriously infringed by the Navy's
vaccine requirements and refused to stay the preliminary injunction.

In another vaccine mandate case, President Biden issued EO 14042 which
required that contractors and subcontractors performing federal contracts
ensured that their employees and others working in connection with federal
contracts were fully vaccinated against COVID-19. Six states, several governors, various state agencies, and the Associated Builders and Contractors,
which represents contractors across the country, challenged the EO. The order
relied upon the Federal Property and Administrative Services Act (40 USC 101)
("the Procurement Act").

In reviewing the Procurement Act, the Eleventh Circuit Court concluded that
it found nothing that contemplates that every executive agency can base every
procurement decision on the health of the contracting workforce. The court
observed that it expected Congress to speak clearly when authorizing an agency
to exercise powers of vast economic and political significance. It declared that
including a COVID-19 requirement in every contract and solicitation, across
broad procurement categories, requires clear congressional authorization.

The court found that an all-encompassing vaccine requirement is different in nature from the sort of project-specific restrictions contemplated in the Act. It declared that like other enabling legislation the statute is not an "open book" to which agencies may "add pages and change the plotline."

The circuit court concluded that no statutory provision contemplated the power to implement an across-the-board vaccine mandate, and the president's authority to issue the EO depended on whether Congress delegated the power to require widespread vaccination through the Procurement Act. The court found that all signs suggested that Congress had retained the power rather than passing it on. It concluded that the plaintiffs were likely to succeed on their claim that the president had exceeded his authority. The Appeals Court limited the injunction to enforcement of the mandate to the parties, which of course included all the members of the nationwide Associated Builders and Contractors (*State of Georgia et. al.* v. *Biden*, US Court of Appeals for the 11th Circuit, No. 21–14769 [8/26/2022] 17–30).

A further COVID-19 related case dealt with housing evictions. In March 2020, Congress passed the Coronavirus Aid, Relief, and Economic Security Act (CARES Act). Among other things, it imposed a 120-day moratorium on evictions for properties that participate in federal assistance programs or were subject to federally backed loans. The moratorium expired in July 2020 and Congress did not renew it. Through the Centers for Disease Control and Prevention (CDC), the Biden administration imposed a new moratorium covering all residential properties nationwide and imposing criminal penalties, which was set to expire on December 31, 2020. Congress extended it for one month. Upon expiration, the CDC extended it through March 2021, then again through June, and then again through July. President Biden stated that the new moratorium would buy time to protect the estimated three million Americans who could face eviction.

The Alabama Association of REALTORS® sued; the district court granted summary judgment holding that the CDC lacked statutory authority to impose the moratorium, and issued a stay on implementation of the moratorium. The Supreme Court took up the issue of whether to remove the stay.

In defending its order, the CDC relied on section 361(a) of the Public Health Service Act of 1944. The Supreme Court observed that the provision had rarely been invoked and never before for an eviction moratorium. Further, the court stated that regulations pursuant to the provision informed the grant of authority by illustrating the kind of measures that could be necessary: inspection, fumigation, disinfection, sanitation, and so on. The court thus concluded that the downstream connection between eviction and the interstate spread of disease was marked by differences from the direct targeting of disease that characterizes the measures identified in the statute (*Alabama Association of Realtors* v. *U.S. Department of Health and Human Services,*

141 S. Ct. 2488 [2021]). Questioning the government's interpretation of the statute, the court declared that it expected Congress to speak clearly when authorizing an agency to exercise power of "vast economic and political significance" and that since the provision's enactment in 1944, no regulation premised on it had even begun to approach the size and scope of the eviction moratorium. The court further pointed out that Congress was on notice that a further extension of the eviction moratorium would require new legislation, yet it had failed to act to extend it. It concluded, "it is up to Congress, not the CDC to decide whether the public interest merits further action here" (141 S. Ct. 2490). The court refused to lift the district court's stay. Following this, President Biden requested that the CDC issue a new scaled-down moratorium just for counties experiencing high COVID-19 case rates. CDC refused, saying it lacked the legal authority to do so.

President Biden also issued an EO affecting state and local education programs. On January 20, 2021, he issued EO 13988 titled "Preventing and Combating Discrimination on the Basis of Gender Identity or Sexual Orientation." In response, the Department of Education issued guidance providing its interpretation of Title IX of the Education Amendments Act of 1972 (86 Fed. Reg. 3267 [June 15, 2021]). The Equal Employment Opportunity Commission (EEOC) issued a "Technical Assistance Document" on June 15, 2021 providing its new interpretation of the Civil Rights act of 1964. The Department of Education's guidance states that the department will fully enforce Title IX to prohibit discrimination based on sexual orientation and gender identity in educational programs and activities that receive federal funding. The EEOC's document purports to explain employers' obligations with respect to dress codes, bathrooms, locker rooms, showers, and use of preferred pronouns or names. It also invites individuals to file a charge of discrimination with the EEOC if they believe their rights under Title VII as explained within the document have been violated. Several states filed a complaint challenging the legality of the documents issued by the department and the EEOC in the response to the president's EO, contending that both were procedurally and substantively unlawful under the APA.

The district court observed that under the APA "legislative rules" require notice and comment rulemaking while "interpretative rules" do not. The government claimed that the documents constituted interpretative rules and that notice and comment procedures were therefore not followed. The court found that the department's guidance "plausibly adopted a new position inconsistent with the Department's existing regulations, supporting the conclusion that the Department's guidance is legislative" (*State of Tennessee v. United States Department of Education* US Dist. Lexis 125684, 58 [2022]). Also, the court found that the EEOC's guidance identified and created rights for applicants and employees that had not been established by federal law, and it directed employers to comply with those obligations to avoid liability (US Dist. Lexis 125684, 62). Therefore, it concluded that the guidance documents were legislative rules, and that the guidance was invalid, because the agencies had failed to comply with the notice and comment procedures of the APA (US Dist. Lexis 125684, 62). The court explained that the public has an interest in agencies promulgating rules that have the effect of law through procedures mandated by Congress (US Dist. Lexis 125684, 64). Accordingly, the distric court issued a preliminary injunction enjoining any implementation of either of the agencies' documents.

A major environmental case was decided by the Supreme Court that has significant ramifications for many policy and administrative areas beyond environmental policy and management of environmental programs. Challenges to a climate change prevention policy initiated to curb greenhouse gases, initiated by President Obama and titled the Clean Power Plan, was decided by the Supreme Court during the Biden administration. The plan included a requirement based on the administration's interpretation of the Clean Air Act that required existing coal-fired power plants to reduce their production of electricity or subsidize increased generation by means of natural gas, wind, or solar energy.

The EPA explained that rather than setting the standard based on the application of equipment and practices at the level of the individual power facility, the Clean Power Plan had instead based the standard on a shift in the energy generation mix at grid level – not the sort of measure that has the potential for application at individual power facilities (*West Virginia* v. *Environmental Protection Agency*, 84 Fed. Reg. 32524 [2022]).

The Biden White House stated that the Clean Power Plan would drive an "aggressive transformation in the domestic energy industry" (*West Virginia* v. *EPA* 597 US___2022, 16).

The regulation was challenged in various district courts. The case in *West Virginia* v. *Environmental Protection Agency* was consolidated with several others for hearing by the Supreme Court. In framing its analysis, the court addressed the applicable section of the Clean Air Act and declared, "The issue here is whether restructuring the Nation's overall mix of electricity generation to transition from 38% coal to 27% coal by 2030 can be the 'best system of emission reduction' within the meaning of Section 111" (*West Virginia* v. *Environmental Protection Agency*, 142 S. Ct. 2587, 2606 [2022]). The Supreme Court observed that the EPA had never devised a cap by looking at a "system" that would reduce pollution simply by "shifting" polluting activity from dirtier to cleaner sources (142 S. Ct. 2609). The court found that there was no control a coal company plant operator could deploy to attain the emissions limits established by the Clean Power Plan (142 S. Ct. 2610).

The court stated that

> Rather than focus on improving the performance of individual sources the Plan would improve the overall power system by lowering the carbon intensity of power generation. And it would do that by forcing a shift throughout the power grid from one type of energy source to another. In the words of the then EPA Administrator, the rule was "not about pollution control" so much as it was "an investment opportunity" for States, especially investments in renewables and clean energy. (142 S. Ct. 2610)

Assessing EPA's stance, the court then declared, "This view of EPA's authority was not only unprecedented; it also effected a fundamental revision of the statute, changing it from one sort of scheme of regulation into an entirely different kind. Under the Agency's prior view of Section 111, its rule was limited to ensuring the efficient pollution performance of each individual regulated source" (142 S. Ct. 2610–2611). Further, the court opined, "On EPA's view of Section 111, Congress implicitly tasked it, and it alone, with balancing the many vital considerations of national policy implicated in deciding how Americans will get their energy" (142 S. Ct. 2613).

In explaining the reasoning for its decision, the Supreme Court used this case to state its stance on evaluating federal agency interpretations of the statutes on which they based their regulations. In doing so, the principle laid down is a culmination and crystallization of the principles it had enunciated in previous cases. In stating the reasoning underlying its analysis for EPA's claimed authority, the court asserted and discussed its "major questions" doctrine. It first laid out the reasoning that underlies the doctrine – reasoning that it had expressed in previous cases, as well. The court explained how it viewed an agency's interpretation of its authorizing statutes:

> Both separation of powers principles and a practical understanding of legislative intent make us reluctant to read into ambiguous statutory text the delegation claimed to be lurking there. To convince us otherwise, something more than a merely plausible textual basis for the agency action is necessary. The agency instead must point to clear congressional authorization for the power it claims. (142 S. Ct. 2608–2609)

As a result, the court went on to declare: "The bottom line of clear congressional authorization confirms our view that the approach under the major questions doctrine is distinct" (142 S. Ct. 2609).

The Supreme Court indicated that the "major questions" doctrine has been gestating for some time, observing: "As for the major questions doctrine, it took hold because it refers to an identifiable body of law that has developed over a particular and recurring problem: agencies asserting highly consequential power beyond what Congress could reasonably be understood to have granted" (142 S. Ct. 2609). The court stated that with regard to the "major questions" doctrine, it had wide applicability. It cited the Supreme Court's recent decision invalidating the Occupational Safety and Health Administration's mandate that 84 million Americans "either obtain a COVID-19 vaccine or undergo weekly medical testing at their own expense" (142 S. Ct. 2608). The court made it clear that it would employ the "major questions" doctrine in cases far beyond the immediate case involving the EPA or even in the environmental arena. The "major questions" doctrine, the court explained, would be employed "in cases in which the history and the breadth of the authority that the agency has asserted, and the economic and political significance of that assertion, provide a reason to hesitate before concluding that Congress meant to confer such an authority" (142 S. Ct. 2608).

The court then applied the doctrine to the EPA case:

> Under our precedents, this is a major questions case. In arguing that Section 11(d) empowers it to substantially restructure the American energy market, EPA claimed to discover in a long-extant statute an unheralded power representing a transformative expansion in its regulatory authority. It located that newfound power in the vague language of an ancillary provision of the Act . . . . And the agency's discovery allowed it to adopt a regulatory program that Congress has conspicuously and repeatedly declined to enact itself. (142 S. Ct. 2609)

The court indicated its skepticism toward the EPA's claim of power and stated that to overcome that skepticism, the agency, under the "major questions" doctrine, would have to point to clear congressional authorization to regulate in the manner it had declared (142 S. Ct. 2613). The Supreme Court concluded: "But it is not plausible that Congress gave EPA the authority to adopt on its own such a regulatory scheme in Section 111(d). A decision of such magnitude and consequence rests with Congress itself, or an agency acting pursuant to a clear delegation from that representative body" (142 S. Ct. 2615).

The Supreme Court proclaims that cases requiring treatment under the "major questions" doctrine have arisen from all corners of the administrative state. One such case that it cited was *Alabama Association of Realtors* v. *Department of Health and Human Services* (discussed earlier in this section) in which the court "concluded that the Centers for Disease Control and Prevention could not, under its authority to adopt measures necessary to prevent the ... spread of disease, institute a nationwide eviction moratorium in response to the COVID-19 pandemic" (141 S. Ct. 2608). By citing this case and several others, including its decision to invalidate the OSHA mandate that eighty-four million Americans obtain a COVID-19 vaccine (as discussed earlier), the court signaled that the "major questions" doctrine will have very wide applicability in its future decisions and in those of the lower courts.

Federal administrative agencies have been put on notice that their claims of authority for issuing regulations will be scrutinized by the federal courts, and if such claims cannot be clearly demonstrated to be authorized in congressionally adopted statutes, the regulations will be declared null and void, regardless of the president's executive directives behind them. The Supreme Court has made it clear that it regards specific congressional authorization as the touchstone for validating agency action, not presidential direction alone.

Subsequently, another Biden directive involved the Federal Student Loan Program. President Biden's directive that the Department of Education should forgive undergraduate tuition-related federal student debt was challenged in federal courts. During his presidential campaign, Biden promised to forgive debts for those with student loans whose earnigs did not exceed $125,000. When he became president, he instructed the Department of Education to prepare a legal memorandum exploring possible legal avenues for justifying a loan-forgiveness program. The Trump administration had considered a program to forgive student loans during the COVID-19 pandemic, and analyzed its authority to do so under the Higher Education Relief for Students Act of 2003 (HEROS Act). The Department of Education concluded at the time that it lacked legal authority to do this. Under Biden, the department reversed course and concluded the HEROS Act did allow such a program, because of the financial harms of the COVID-19 pandemic. Whereupon, the White House announced that the president would fulfill his campaign commitment by providing debt forgiveness to millions of borrowers (The White House 2022). The secretary of education, invoking his authority under the HEROS Act, provided notice of the debt waivers and modifications in the Federal Register. It provided debt relief for individuals earning under $125,000 (or $250,000 if married) and who had Direct Perkins or Federal Family Education Loans, which are not commercially held. The program provided $20,000 in debt forgiveness to Pell Grant recipients and 10,000 to nonrecipients.

Six states sued, claiming that the plan exceeded the secretary's authority. The Supreme Court took up the case on appeal. The court pointed out that the

HEROS Act provided that the secretary may issue waivers in connection with a war or other military operation or a national emergency. The court observed that the Department of Education had estimated that about forty-three million borrowers would qualify for relief and the Congressional Budget Office estimated that the plan would cancel $430 billion in debt and principal. It declared, "The authority to 'modify' statutes and regulations allows the Secretary to make modest adjustments and additions to existing provisions, not transform them" (*Biden* v. *Nebraska*, 2023, Slip op. 13). The court concluded that the secretary had gone far beyond modest adjustments:

> The Secretary's new "modifications" of these provisions were not "moderate" or "minor." Instead, he created a novel and fundamentally different loan forgiveness program ... From a few narrowly delineated situations specified by Congress, the Secretary has expanded forgiveness to nearly every borrower in the country. The Secretary's plan has "modified" the cited provisions only in the same sense that the French revolution modified the status of the French nobility – it has abolished them with a new regime entirely. (*Biden* v. *Nebraska*, 2023, Slip op. 16)

The court went on to characterize the secretary's actions as follows: "What the Secretary has actually done is draft a new section of the Education Act from scratch by 'waiving' provisions root and branch and then filling the empty space with a radically new text" (*Biden* v. *Nebraska*, 2023, Slip op. 17).

The Supreme Court did not declare that loan forgiveness could not be done under any circumstances. It called attention to its approach in recent cases in which the extent of the interpretation of federal statutes had been in question. "The question here is not whether something should be done: it is who has the authority to do it. Our recent decision in West Virginia v. EPA involved similar concerns over the exercise of administrative power" (*Biden* v. *Nebraska*, 2023, Slip op. 19). It will be recalled that in that case, the court evoked the "major questions" doctrine in which it declared that it would judge administrative statutory interpretations and the resultant administrative actions by the degree to which they entailed major economic and political significance. Here, the court concluded,

> The "economic and political significance" of the Secretary's action is staggering by any measure. A budget model issued by the Wharton School of the University of Pennsylvania estimates that the program will cost taxpayers between $469 and $519 billion depending on the total number of borrowers ultimately covered. That is ten times the "economic impact" that we found significant in concluding that an eviction moratorium implemented by the Centers for Disease Control and Prevention triggered the major questions doctrine. (*Biden* v. *Nebraska*, 2023, Slip op. 21)

With regard to the primacy of Congress's authority, the court even quoted the Democratic speaker of the house: "As then–Speaker of the House Nancy Pelosi explained: 'people think the President of the United States has the power for debt foregiveness. He does not. He can postpone. He can delay. But he does not have that power. That has to be an act of Congress'" (*Biden* v. *Nebraska*, 2023, Slip op. 23). The court then stated, "All this leads us to conclude that the basic and consequential tradeoffs inherent in a mass debt cancellation program are ones that Congress would likely have intended for itself" (*Biden* v. *Nebraska*, 2023, Slip op. 24). Finally, it declared, "We hold today that the HEROS Act allows the Secretary to 'waive' or 'modify' existing statutory or regulatory provisions applicable to financial assistance provisions, not to transform them" (*Biden* v. *Nebraska*, 2023, Slip op. 13).

Thus, the Supreme Court has repeatedly emphasized the importance of the "major questions" doctrine in three major decisions in different areas of policy. As such, it is emphatic in its insistence that presidential directives and agency actions should not stray too far from the dictates embodied in statutes passed by Congress.

6 The Impact and Implications of Federal Court Actions on Presidential Directives

As discussed in Section 1, the major question addressed in this analysis has been to what extent the federal courts have declared support for or restraint on presidential directives by modern presidents. Relatedly, to what extent has support or restraint increased or decreased? A second question that has been considered is: What are the major bases or principles the courts have relied upon and enunciated in their decisions? This is important as it signals the kind of treatment future presidential directives and agency administrative actions may receive from the federal courts.

The following is a summary of federal judicial decisions, with brief summaries of presidential directives, categorized according to whether they were supportive, mixed, or restrictive of presidential directives.

Supportive

Abraham Lincoln
- *Military tribunal tries an American Citizen without recourse to ordinary courts*: Supreme Court declares it does not have jurisdiction over military commission.
- *Lincoln orders blockade of southern ports*: Supreme Court declares the president possesses the whole executive power and can act without waiting for any special legislative authority.

Theodore Roosevelt

- *Multiple wide-ranging orders*: Little pushback from Congress or courts.

Woodrow Wilson

- *Multiple wide-ranging orders*: Little pushback from Congress or courts.

Franklin Roosevelt

- *Multiple wide-ranging orders*: For example, *EO resulting in Japanese Americans being detained in relocation centers*: Approved by Supreme Court in *Korematsu*; *Curtiss-Wright*: "sole organ doctrine" pronounced.

Harry Truman

- *EO seizing coal mines:* Approved in *United States* v. *United Mine Workers of America* – commander in chief authority cited by Supreme Court.

Richard Nixon

- *Military orders sending troops to Vietnam*: Courts employ political question doctrine – nonjusticiable issue, separation of powers.

William Clinton

- *Military order for US military to participate in NATO operations in Yugoslavia*: Petition by several congressmen alleging the order violated the Constitution's War Powers Clause refused by the court because the whole of Congress had not acted using the tools available to it.

Donald Trump

- *Third EO limiting entry into United States of those from eight countries whose governments maintain inadequate information about citizens*: Court rules worldwide multiagency review supports president's finding that those entrants would be detrimental to US interests.
- *President directs Department of Defense to transfer $2.5 billion for border wall projects*: Ruling that plaintiffs have no cause for action to bring a suit.

Joe Biden

- *Mandate requiring medical facilities receiving funds under Medicare and Medicaid to ensure workers are vaccinated for COVID-19*: Ruling that agency's regulation mandating vaccination is authorized in statute.

Mixed

Abraham Lincoln

- *Order suspending habeas corpus*: Supreme Court issues writ for seized person; Lincoln ingnores writ. No further action by the court.

Jimmy Carter/Ronald Reagan

- *EOs blocking transfer of Iran's property*: Congress implicitly approved settlement of claims by executive agreement, but president does not have plenary authority to settle claims.

Ronald Reagan

- *EOs require agency regulatory planning process and cost–benefit analysis before issuing rules*: Agency can comply with both EO and APA, but indefinite postponement of rule requires notice and comment procedures. Agency's failure to issue a notice of proposed regulation is an unreasonable delay under the APA.

George H. W. Bush

- *Military order to send troops to Saudi Arabia*: Congressional approval required if Congress desires to become involved. For purposes of the constitutional War Clause, courts have the ability to make factual and legal determinatios. Judicial determination is premature since Congress has not decided whether war declaration is necessary.

Barack Obama

- *President's position that provision of Foreign Relations Authorization Act, allowing citizens born in Jerusalem to list birthplace as Israel, does not change federal policy*: Court rules that while president's power in foreign relations is not umlimited, the president alone has the right to recognize foreign countries. Pares back "sole organ doctrine"; president is not free from Congress's lawmaking powers.

Restrictive

George Washington

- *Neutrality Proclamation*: Jurors acquit man prosecuted for violating order citing separation of powers.

John Adams

- *Order to seize ships from French courts*: Supreme Court invalidates – congressional acts superior to EOs.

Abraham Lincoln

- *Military tribunal tries a US citizen for conspiracy*: Supreme Court declares all trials shall be by jury and military commission trial was a violation of law.

Harry Truman

- *EO seizing steel mills disapproved in Youngstown*: Separation of powers cited by the Supreme Court.

Richard Nixon

- *Electronic surveillance of citizens for national security*: President's national security responsibilities are not sufficient to preclude requirement of judicial approval of surveillance.
- *Presidential impoundment of funds appropriated by Congress*: President cannot allot funds less than the amount appropriated without the approval of Congress; separation of powers.

William Clinton

- *EO prohibits federal contractors from employing striker replacements*: Order violates NLRA. Presidential action does not insulate the entire executive branch from judicial review.
- *Under the Line Item Veto Act, president cancels one budget provision and two tax provisions passed by Congress*: Court declares both Act and president's actions violate Article I of the Constitution.

George W. Bush

- *Citizen captured in Afghanistan detained in Guantanamo as an enemy combatant*: President's power to conduct foreign affairs does not exclude judicial action where civil liberties are implicated.
- *Military order establishing military tribunal to try citizens who provided assistance in 9/11 attacks on the basis of claimed inherent presidential authority*: Court rules Military Commission's structure and procedures violate the UCMJ and four Geneva Conventions.
- *Foreign national captured abroad and detained at Guantanamo without right to habeas corpus*: Court rules that just as with citizens, aliens are entitled to habeas corpus.
- *Foreign nationals accused of being members of Al-Qaeda designated as enemy combatants and denied habeas corpus under Provisions of Military Commission Act*: Court declares Act effected an unconstitutional suspension of habeas corpus – judicial redress is crucial to balancing powers in separation of powers.
- *EO prohibiting federal agencies from requiring PLAs for construction contracts pursuant to president's power to faithfully execute the laws*: Court holds order violates the NLRA and exceeds president's constitutional and statutory authority.

Barack Obama

- *President's program to defer prosecution for those in the United States illegally who are parents of permanent residents*: Court rules program violates APA.

Donald Trump

- *EO that sanctuary cities not cooperating with federal authorities are ineligible to receive federal grants*: Court rules order violates separation of powers. Congress's Spending Clause power – no inherent executive power to condition funds on president's priorities. Violates Tenth Amendment.
- *First EO limiting entry of aliens from seven countires*: Ruling that president's powers over foreign relations is not unbounded – subject to other branches' actions to protect civil liberties.
- *Second EO travel ban – ban no longer applies to green card and valid visa holders or Iraq entrants*: Ruling that president must have a definitive finding that entrants constitute harm to the United States.
- *Repeal of DACA program which allowed noncitizens who entered the United Staes as children to apply for deferred action from deportation*: Ruling that the decision is deficient under the APA and must go through its processes.

Joe Biden

- *Mandate for private employers who employ over 100 employees to require COVID-19 vaccination of employees*: Ruling that administration may not extend regulatory authority under OSHA without congressional authorization.
- *Mandate for Department of Defense Employees (Navy Seals) to be vaccinated for COVID-19*: Ruling that mandate violates RFRA.
- *Mandate that all government contractors must require employee COVID-19 vaccination*: Ruling that order is not within the authority of the Procurement Act.
- *Moratorium on eviction of renters for COVID-19 emergency*: Ruling that administration's interpretation of the Health Services Act is invalid – exceeded congressional authorization.
- *President's appointment of members of NLRB pursuant to rationale of congressional recess*: Ruling that appointments violate the Constitution's Recess Clause.
- *EO to mandate gender equity in education*: Ruling that the rules issued violate the procedures required by the APA.
- *New rules applied to utilities pursuant to the Clean Power Plan*: Ruling that the regulations exceed the agency's authority under the Clean Air Act; interpretation of the agency's regulatory authority assessed by the Supreme Court under its "major questions" doctrine.
- *EO to forgive college undergraduate students' loan debt*: Ruling that action has no statutory authorization under the HEROS Act and Supreme Court's "major questions" doctrine.

What may seem surprising is that at the beginning of the nation, when the US Constitution was just being implemented, the judiciary started out in restrictive mode with judgments going against decisions of the first two presidents. As presented in Table 1, however, for many later presidents – and particularly during the presidencies of Lincoln, Theodore Roosevelt, Woodrow Wilson, and Franklin Roosevelt, who issued directives on a wide range of matters with far reaching impacts on American society – the courts were largely either inactive in significantly challenging presidential authority when issuing directives, or actively supported it. The high point of support or the low point for restraint may have been the Korematsu case involving the relocation and detention of Japanese Americans during Franklin Roosevelt's administration. Subsequently, Chief Justice Roberts, writing for the majority in *Hawaii* v. *Trump* declared, "Korematsu was gravely wrong the day it was decided, has been overruled in the court of history, and to be clear, has no place in law under the Constitution" (138 St. Ct. 2423 [2018]).

The Supreme Court moved toward some partial restraint during the Truman administration in the Youngstown steel seizure case after previously approving Truman's seizure of coal mines, but the opinion in Youngstown was compromised by several concurring opinions that in some ways supported independent presidential power. The support–restriction picture became more mixed during the Nixon Aadministration. While several challenges to Nixon's orders involving Vietnam War miliary movements were turned down by the federal judiciary, the administration's national security claims that undergirded intelligence collection involving American citizens were turned down in a case invoking civil liberties. In addition, Nixon's budget impoundment initiative was thwarted on separation of powers grounds.

The Carter, Reagan, and H. W. Bush administrations' experiences with the federal judiciary were mixed, with rulings that permitted presidential directives, but at the same time placed limits on them. The Clinton administration's orders directing military actions were not turned down on grounds similar to the judiciary's treatment of Nixon's military orders – that is, on standing grounds – because the whole Congress had not challenged them, only a subset had. However, in the domestic arena, the Clinton administration faced significant judicial pushback and one of his EOs was completely voided.

More recent presidents have experienced even more judicial pushback. George W. Bush's terrorist control initiatives experienced a series of defeats in federal courts, as did his domestic labor relations initiative. President Obama received a positive decision in a diplomatic recognition case, but the Supreme Court paired back the "sole organ doctrine" that had been cited numerous times before in previous cases to support presidential actions in dealing with foreign affairs. A major Obama immigration policy was wholly rejected on procedural grounds by the court. Also with regard to immigration policy, Donald Trump experienced major defeats in attempting to restrict entry into the United States by foreign nationals, and he was forced to significantly modify his initiative in the face of judicial opposition. Relatedly, his attempt to repeal the previous administration's DACA program was turned down on procedural grounds similar to those used in Obama's defeat. Trump did register one victory: his decision to reprogram budget funds for his border wall initiative.

Joe Biden issued several directives mandating COVID-19 vaccinations for most sectors of American society and experienced defeat for all but one of them, largely on grounds that they exceed the statutory authority specified by Congress. Likewise, his moratorium on the eviction of renters on account of the COVD-19 pandemic was also rejected. Other major initiatives across a swath of domestic policy areas also experienced rejection including labor relations, gender equity in education, college student-loan forgiveness, and environmental regulation of utilities. This last case in which the administration's Clean Power Plan was rejected brought a judicial doctrine that portends support for judicial challenges to presidential directives and agency regulatory initiatives across a wide range of domestic policies. In sum, modern presidents have experienced more restrictive decisions from the federal courts over their directives than previous presidents did.

The bases and principles enunciated by the federal courts for supporting or restricting presidential directives are important, as they have implications for the direction and breadth of judicial treatment of presidential directives in the future. During the terms of the first two presidents, the federal courts established the principle that separation of powers matters, emphasizing that legislative power belongs to Congress and congressional final acts are superior to presidential directives alone. The federal judiciary's decisions concerning Lincoln's actions during the Civil War were mixed, but the Supreme Court was supportive of his use of military tribunals to try American citizens by disavowing jurisdiction and was also supportive of his military blockade of southern ports under his powers as commander in chief.

During Franklin Roosevelt's administration, the claim of inherent presidential authority as commander in chief to issue military directives, even those directly impacting American citizens, perhaps achieved its high watermark in the case involving the detention of Japanese Americans. Similarly, Roosevelt's appointment of military tribunals to try nationals of nations at war with the United States was affirmed by the Supreme Court, which recognized the president's inherent authority as commander in chief to perform functions which may constitutionally be performed by the military in times of war. The authority of the commander in chief rationale received further support in the case involving Roosevelt's appointment of military tribunals. The president's inherent authority to conduct foreign affairs was given further credence in the Curtiss-Wright case, where the Supreme Court's declaration in dicta of the "sole organ doctrine," even though it was not critical to the decision in the case itself, was nonetheless endorsed in subsequent cases.

The inherent authority of the president as commander in chief experienced something of a setback in the steel mills seizure case during the Truman administration, but as discussed in Section 2, the Supreme Court's declaration that the commander in chief's power to take private property did not comport with the US Constitution and that such a power belonged to Congress was compromised by several concurring opinions. The president's authority as commander in chief to direct military operations, as related to Congress's war-declaring power, was tested several times during the Nixon administration but the challenges largely ultimately failed on grounds of the plaintiffs' lack of standing, without the courts ruling on the merits. The courts were unsympathetic to suits brought by individuals on the grounds that such issues were political questions, and they were unsympathetic to individual congressional representatives or groups of representatives on the grounds that such suits, on a separation of powers issue, must be brought by the "whole Congress." The whole Congress principle received further support from the courts during the H. W. Bush and Clinton administrations. The Supreme Court also invoked the "political question" doctrine to indicate that the methods and means by which the two political branches together wind down a conflict is beyond the power and competency of the judiciary. However, the court did affirm the principle that courts do not lack the power to make factual and legal determinations of whether the nation's military actions constitute war for purposes of the constitutional War Clause.

Beyond presidential directives regarding the engagement of military forces, the president's national security power when it comes to the impact on individual rights and liberties has faced significant limitations since the Roosevelt administration. The Truman steel seizure case was a minor example, but subsequent presidential actions have been met with further judicial limitations. Electronic eavesdropping by intelligence agencies was met by the Supreme Court with the principle that such authority must receive prior judicial approval to be valid, and the Nixon administration's separation of powers arguments were not accepted. The court insisted, instead, on judicial approval for such action to be valid.

Court cases during the George W. Bush administration further strengthened the principle that when it comes to civil liberties, the president's national security authority and separation of powers argument is no bar to the judiciary asserting the primacy of constitutional rights and liberties, such as the right of habeas corpus. Trump's immigration orders also faced significant judicial pushback. The administration's inherent authority argument that the president's actions were unreviewable by the judiciary because they were motivated by his national security responsibility was rejected by the courts. Instead, it was declared that the courts, as a regular matter, are entitled to review the constitutionality of actions taken by the executive to promote national security and even invalidate them, including in times of conflict. However, the Supreme Court's review of Trump's third entry ban found a well-documented, scaled-back process that complied with the statute, and it was thus approved. The court exercised its right to review the president's directive but validated it when it followed the statute.

With regard to domestic policy decisions, the judiciary has asserted limitations on presidential directives for which the courts found violations of the separation of powers through the executive exercising powers allocated by the US Constitution to Congress. Both the Clinton and George W. Bush directives involving labor policy were declared to exceed presidential constitutional and statutory authority and encroach on Congress's power. It was declared that presidential action does not bar the entire executive branch from judicial review.

The judiciary has also emphasized that the president's budgetary authority is not unlimited. In both the Nixon and Clinton administrations, the courts disallowed unilateral budgetary decisions taken without the participation of Congress. The judiciary declared that the presidents' actions violated the separation of powers and the requirement that laws, including budget laws, must proceed through the entire lawmaking process that the US Constitution prescribes. Relatedly, Trump's attempt to modify funding allocations to so-called sanctuary cities violated Congress's constitutional Spending Clause power, and the courts found that there is no inherent executive power to condition funds on presidential priorities.

The judiciary has increasingly stressed that presidential directives do not serve to bar judicial oversight and judgment regarding the processes prescribed by presidential directives or those used by agencies to implement such directives. Rather, the courts have scrutinized such processes and procedures to assess their conformance with constitutional and statutory law. For example, the courts made it clear that Reagan's agency regulatory planning requirements would not be allowed to obviate agency responsibilities to follow the processes required by the APA. Similarly, Obama's immigration order to defer prosecution of illegal immigrants who were the parents of permanent residents who were brought to the United States illegally as children, and Trump's attempt to repeal Obama's DACA order, were both declared violative of the APA.

During the Biden administration, the judiciary emphasized that it was going to assiduously review presidents' and their subordinates' claims of statutory authority undergirding presidential directives. With regard to Biden's COVID-19 mandate orders, the courts concluded that the administration's interpretation of the Occupational Health and Safety Act, the Health Services Act, and the Procurement Act were all invalid, and one violated the Religious Freedom Restoration Act. Only one directive, the COVID-19 vaccination mandate for health workers, was found in conformance with the statute. The judiciary declared that executive agencies are the creations of statute, and accordingly only possess the authority Congress has provided; therefore, it expected Congress to speak clearly when authorizing agencies to exercise powers of vast economic and political significance. This "speak clearly" principle was expanded and consolidated in the Supreme Court's opinion in *West Virginia* v. *EPA* in which the court proclaimed its "major questions" doctrine. It made it very clear that the federal courts are to employ this doctrine in cases in which the history and breadth of the authority that the agencies assert, and the economic and political significance of the assertion, provide a reason to hesitate before concluding that Congress meant to confer such authority.

The Supreme Court considers the "major questions" doctrine to have wide applicability across government, citing its decision to strike down Biden's COVID-19 vaccine mandate for private sector workers as an example. Additionally, as discussed in Section 5, the Supreme Court invalidated Biden's loan-forgiveness directive in the education arena, emphasizing the application of the "major questions" doctrine. The doctrine poses a major bar not only for president's directive actions, but also for federal agencies across the board which overreach the authority explicitly provided by Congress. The court has signaled that a president's directive, by itself, is no help to agencies if a court finds that their interpretation of the congressional authority granted to them violates the "major questions" doctrine.

Numerous scholars and analysts have observed and been critical of the fact that, for a considerable period of time, the federal courts had generally displayed a supportive posture toward presidential directives. They permitted expansive interpretations of both constitutional and statutory provisions to justify such directives. For recent presidents, however, this posture has begun to shift. In the cases reviewed here, the courts have enunciated more exacting principles and have used them to overturn presidential directives. In particular, the Supreme Court has pronounced a significantly consequential principle with its "major questions" doctrine.

A major factor in the increasingly successful challenges to presidential directives is the increased activity of states in challenging them in federal court. In order to defeat a presidential directive, they do not have to challenge an EO directly (although that has been done successfully, as illustrated by the voiding of Clinton's EO on striker replacements). States can instead directly challenge the agency actions undertaken pursuant to the president's directives.

State attorneys general have been in the forefront of challenges to presidential directives. Their activity in mounting challenges in federal courts has been facilitated by the National Association of Attorneys General. The association promotes litigation by having members participate in working groups that focus on potential multistate lawsuits. It offers "lead" states the opportunity to recruit other states to join specific litigation. It also offers grants to states to get litigation off the ground. The prominence of coordinated multistate lawsuits to challenge federal policy is a relatively recent phenomenon. While states have a long history of suing the federal government in federal courts, and have had some success in doing so, these were typically single state efforts. More recently, partisan coalitions of attorneys general have used multistate lawsuits as a way to block federal policies and to prompt federal action.

This multistate litigation activity against the federal government can be seen in statistics of the cases brought against the Obama, Trump, and Biden administrations. The statistics show that multistate litigation is largely (but not exclusively) led by attorneys general of the party that is opposite to the president's party. For the Obama administration, there were 78 multistate suits with 58 led by Republican attorneys general, 11 led by Democrats, and 9 that were bipartisan led. For the Trump administration, there were 159 multistate lawsuits with 155 led by Democrat attorneys general, 4 by Republicans, and 0 bipartisan. With respect to the Biden administration, in a little over his first two years in office there were 60 lawsuits with 54 led by Republican attorneys general, 3 by Democrats, and 3 were bipartisan (National Association of Attorneys General, 2023). The Trump administration experienced the most suits overall, but Biden has only been in office for about one-half of one term at the time of writing. If the trend continues, the Biden administration will exceed the Obama total. The Obama administration had the largest number of attorneys general from his own party leading the suits or joining in bipartisan led suits.

State challenges to federal executive actions have also recently been facilitated by federal court decisions granting states standing to sue to force or halt administrative actions. As Davis (2019, 1233) observes, "State standing to sue the federal government for financial injuries is the new public standing." This development has, in many respects, channeled public interest litigation through the states, making state governments the new public interest litigants; and it has channeled high-profile public interest litigation through the offices of state attorneys general (Davis, 2019, 1303). The expanded policymaking role of state attorneys general fits a pattern of polarized politics, as partisan coalitions of attorneys general are increasingly willing to sue the federal government – and their prominent policymaking power is unlikely to lessen anytime soon (Nolette and Provost, 2018). In such cases, federal district courts have often issued nationwide injunctions staying federal action, citing the necessary prevention of irreparable harm and the limits of other forms of aggregate relief (Amdur and Hausman, 2017).

The Supreme Court has made it clear that it is not reluctant to engage in judicial review of executive actions that are challenged by states. It will grant standing to state challengers if they can show that they will suffer a direct harm and/or they can prove violations of procedures such as those of the APA. As demonstrated in several of the cases discussed in this Element, the courts are quite willing to consider a wide variety of harms that the states claim in their suits against federal agencies.

Expansive interpretations of legislation will certainly face challenges based on grounds that Congress did not "plainly state" that the activity was covered by legislation. The "major questions" doctrine will undoubtedly be invoked by states and other plaintiffs who assert that in implementing particular programs and adopting certain regulations federal agencies have overreached their authority, and accordingly, plaintiffs will request federal courts to issue injunctions to stop their implementation. While this development poses a significant limitation on executive power as a whole, including that of the president, it may serve to increase the lawmaking power and responsibility of Congress. It acts as a limitation on presidents who claim nothing more than broad constitutional provisions to justify expansive interpretations of federal domestic program statutes to validate executive directives with wide-ranging impacts on the public. It also acts as a restraint on federal agencies who seek to use broad statements in congressionally passed legislation to adopt specific regulations or take specific actions affecting the public that Congress did not delineate specifically in the legislation.

Conclusion

This Element has charted the evolution of federal court treatment of presidential directives over the history of the United States and illuminated the bases and principles federal courts have used to assess such directives. As discussed, the country has experienced varying levels of activity when it comes to presidential directives. The federal courts have varied their approach to presidential directives – from acceptance to mixed support to restraint. Presidential directives began to get more aggressive during the Clinton and George W. Bush administrations and the federal courts issued more restraining decisions, with one of Clinton's orders completely nullified.

Recent presidents have issued more aggressive directives and the Supreme Court has reacted and issued decisions rejecting the actions and enunciating principles that serve to broadly limit presidential space to issue directives affecting other areas of activity. In short, as recent presidents have taken a lot more overt actions by executive directives, the federal courts have had much more to consider and have more often rejected those aggressive presidential actions on constitutional and statutory grounds.

The restrictions are not equal across all areas of policy. Presidents enjoy more flexibility when it comes to directing military moves, for example, but even with respect to national security, when directives have impinged on civil liberties the courts have stated their responsibility to assert judicial power to restrict directives. Taken as a whole, more recent judicial pronouncements constitute a higher level of restriction than that which pertained previously.

So where does that leave public administrators? As a result of federal judicial decisions, federal public administrators are now operating within a new decision-making environment when it comes to presidential directives The federal judiciary's more skeptical stance regarding the exercise of presidential and agency authority affects administrators' calculations regarding proposing, implementing, and reacting to presidential directives.

When it comes to proposing new presidential directives, or supporting those proposed by interest groups or other agencies, the courts' new assertiveness is likely to shift influence more toward legal staff within agencies and to the Department of Justice – and the opinions of these staff are likely to weigh more heavily in decisions than the program implementers and policy experts. In the clearance process for proposing new directives, additional emphasis will be placed on the assessments of agency general counsels and those of the Department of Justice who can advise on the likelihood of federal court acceptance or rejection. Administrators considering new presidential directives will be well served by consulting the legal staff prior to recommending new presidential actions. The president's staff, too, should be diligent in insisting that presidential directives, whatever the source, are subject to the clearance process to avoid the potential for a federal court override after a presidential directive has been issued.

Agency leaders will also need to factor potential court challenges into their consideration of whether or not to support or oppose proposed presidential directives authored by others. A decision to support a directive based on policy desirability alone will ill serve the president if a successful court challenge is likely to succeed. The implication of the Supreme Court's "major questions" doctrine is that expansion of the reach of federal policies and programs established under existing statutes belongs in the province of Congress. Federal courts are likely to scrutinize skeptically claims of presidential authority as the basis for substantial alteration of existing programs. Agency leaders need to be prepared to suggest that wide-ranging policy change proposals should be submitted to Congress.

Agency implementation is affected as well. Once a presidential directive is issued, an agency (or agencies) responsible for implementing it will begin drafting instructions and/or regulations for implementation. Agency administrators need to be cognizant that any opponents external to the federal government that oppose the new policy are likely to file judicial challenges to the regulations and/or to the process for developing and implementing them.

Agency personnel formulating regulations need to be aware that any regulations straying too far from past interpretations of statutes may be deemed by the federal courts as an agency drafting a new amended statute without congressional approval. The Supreme Court decided exactly that in evaluating the EPA's amended regulations for the Clean Air Act as it applied to utilities, as well as the Department of Education's loan-forgiveness program. The "major questions" doctrine applies to agency regulations just as much as it does to presidential directives.

Agency administrators must also be rigorous in following proper procedures when drafting and promulgating new regulations pursuant to a presidential directive. While agency leaders may feel the imperative to rapidly implement a presidential directive (the president heads the executive branch and is their leader), these leaders could find that rapid decision-making is not certain to lead to rapid implementation. Nonetheless, the federal courts have made it clear that presidents lack authority to bypass congressionally enacted procedures, and derivatively, so do administrative agencies. A federal court disallowed the order of the secretary of the Department of Homeland Security implementing President Obama's DAPA program on grounds that it violated the APA. Similarly, during the Trump administration, the decision of the secretary of the Department of Homeland Security to discontinue the DACA policy was disallowed by the Supreme Court as violative of the APA.

The federal courts have also made it clear that agency officials may not exceed their congressionally enacted statutory authority in administering programs. A federal court disallowed the action by President Trump's attorney general to restrict the receipt of federal grant funds to so-called sanctuary cities, finding that the provisions of the Byrne law did not give him authority to impose conditions that required local officials to assist federal agencies in immigration enforcement.

Once a presidential directive is issued, administrators have to decide how to react to it. As indicated at the beginning of this Element, officials at both federal level and at state and local levels have to decide whether to support or oppose a directive. Potential judicial action weighs in their decision. As mentioned, state officials in particular have become increasingly active in filing federal judicial court challenges against presidential directives and/or federal agency implementing regulations. State attorneys general have banded together to file and argue legal challenges. They have often been successful as federal courts have increasingly found that states have standing to sue, because the courts have found that states will incur costs and injuries as a result of presidential directives. Such judicial findings can be expected to further incentivize state officials to file judicial challenges in the future.

Going forward, presidents may have to be more circumspect in the range of executive directives that they contemplate. They cannot assume that the federal courts will accept broad claims of executive inherent power and must be prepared to cite more specific bases of executive authority stated in the US Constitution or in statutes. They may have to reconsider ambitious directives with large impacts on the citizenry in favor of more negotiation with Congress.

Concomitantly, representatives in Congress should be prepared to consider the specificity of legislation that it adopts when it comes to delegation of authority to agencies. Congressional committees may have to spend more effort specifying the range of activities they delegate to agencies and be more specific about these delegations. Congress may also need to review already enacted legislation to determine whether the delegations contained in it are sufficient to achieve the objectives it now intends. This may entail more difficult negotiations among members with differing views; broader legislative language has often been used as a way to paper over differences.

In Section 1 it was noted that some scholars have argued that the favoring of presidential action by the governmental system as a whole promotes regulatory effectiveness and provides dynamism and energy in administration. They argue that the president can act without the indecision and inefficiency that often characterizes the behavior of collective entities, and can synchronize and apply general principles to agency action in a way that congressional committees, interest groups, and bureaucrats cannot.

Collaborative governance scholars, however, would challenge such assertions and point out that such a top-down management paradigm has been refuted by extensive collaborative public management research (Blomgren-Bingham and O'Leary, 2016). Collaborative research finds that collaboration as opposed to sole actor directives is essential to developing, and especially to implementing, effective public policies. As one researcher opined, "Collaboration has now become the predominant approach to solving complex public problems" (Silvia, 2018, 472).

A basic tenet of collaborative governance is that because the American governmental system provides multiple venues and opportunities for multiple participants – Congress, bureaucrats, interest groups, state and local officials – to determine whether a given policy will be effective, collaboration among the relevant participants in arriving at a policy decision is necessary to achieve policy implementation. The case of President Clinton's federalism EO 13083, in which he listed nine circumstances in which federal action instead of state action was preferable, justifies the collaborative argument. House Majority Leader Armey protested that Clinton acted without any regard to state constitutional prerogatives and had undermined the American constitutional structure. In doing so, Clinton circumnavigated Congress. The order was rejected in the House of Representatives by a vote of 417:2, illustrating the collaborative argument that in the American governmental system, solitary action by any one player provokes a counterreaction by other players that raises the risk the policy becoming ineffectual. Challenges in the courts, as discussed in this Element, are other examples. This phenomenon, of course, represents the Founders' intention when they devised the separation of powers system.

This does not mean that all presidential directives are doomed to be ineffective. However, as noted in Section 1, presidents who want their directives to succeed need to get better at bargaining. In short, a collaborative approach may serve presidents better than a sole actor approach.

These judicial developments provide further lines of inquiry for public administration scholars as well as presidential scholars. Presidential scholars may initiate discussions about the bases for presidential actions and also the boundaries of presidential authority. What do the limitations the federal judiciary places on presidential directives portend for the exercise of presidential authority? What are the costs and benefits for decisive action by presidents? Is the theory of inherent presidential authority dead? If so, what flexibility will future presidents enjoy in directing federal action?

Public administration scholars may investigate how the judiciary's pronouncements will change agency rulemaking. The also may want to trace the limitations on administrators' discretion caused by the judicial principles now being employed by the federal courts. Another potential area for inquiry is how federal jurisprudence is changing the relationship between the presidency and federal agencies.

The federal courts have created a much altered legal environment for presidential directives and administrative actions. Further judicial decisions will reveal just how much impact this will have on presidential authority and administrative discretion.

References

Amdur, S. & Hausman, D. (2017). Nationwide Injunctions and Nationwide Harm. *Harvard Law Review Forum*, 131(2), 49–53.

Armey, D. (1998, August 5). Stop Clinton's Order That Ran Roughshod over Our Constitution. *Atlanta Constitution*, A(5).

Bennet, J. (1998, July 5). True to Form, Clinton Shifts Energies Back to U.S. Focus. *New York Times*.

Biden, J. (2021). Remarks on the COVID-19 Response and National Vaccination Efforts. *Daily Compilation of Presidential Documents*, 775(2). https://bit.ly/3V2WMyO.

Biskupic, J. (2009). *American Original: The Life and Constitution of Antonin Scalia*. New York: Sarah Crichton Books.

Black, H. C. (1979). *Black's Law Dictionary*. Eagan, MN: West Publishing Co.

Blomgren-Bingham, L. & O'Leary, R. (2016). *The Collaborative Public Manager*. Washington, DC: Georgetown University Press.

Branum, T. (2002). President or King? The Use and Abuse of Executive Orders in Modern-Day America. *Journal of Legislation*, 28(1), 1–86.

Calabresi, S. & Prakash, S. (1994). The President's Power to Execute the Laws. *Yale Law Journal*, 104(3), 541–665.

Calabresi, S. & Rhodes, K. (1992). The Structural Constitution: Unitary Executive, Plural Judiciary. *Harvard Law Review*, 105(6), 1153–1205.

Calabresi, S. & Saikrichna, P. K. (1994). The President's Power to Execute the Laws. *Yale Law Journal*, 104(2), 541–665.

Calabresi, S. & Yoo, C. (2008). *The Unitary Executive: Presidential Power from Washington to Bush*. New Haven, CT: Yale University Press.

Clinton, W. (1998). Remarks on Medicare and the Legislative Agenda and an Exchange with Reporters. *Weekly Compilation of Presidential Documents*, 1329.

Committee on Government Operations, 85th Congress. (1957). Executive Orders and Proclamations: A Study of a Use of Presidential Powers. 14th Committee Print, Washington, DC. https://lccn.loc.gov/58060398.

Cooper, P. (2001). The Law, Presidential Memorandum and Executive Orders: Of Patchwork Quilts and Shell Games. *Presidential Studies Quarterly*, 31, 6–14.

Davis, S. (2019). The New Public Standing. *Stanford Law Review*, 71(2), 1229–1304.

Dellinger, W. (2006, June 30). A Supreme Court Conversation. *Slate*. www.slate.com/id/2144476.

Devins, N. & Fisher, L. (2002). The Steel Seizure Case: One of a Kind? *Constitutional Commentary*, 19(1), 63–86.

Entin, J. (1997). The Dog That Rarely Bites: Why the Courts Won't Resolve the War Powers Debate. *Case Western Reserve Law Review*, 47(4), 1305–1315.

Fisher, L. (1975). *Presidential Spending Power*. Princeton, NJ: Princeton University Press.

Fisher, L. (2004). *The Politics of Executive Privilege*. Durham, NC: Carolina Academic Press.

Fisher, L. (2010). The Unitary Executive and the Inherent Power. *University of Pennsylvania Journal of Constitutional Law*, 12(3), 569–596.

Fisher, L. (2013, November 18). Getting It Wrong Again and Again – Judicial Error's Compounding Effects. *National Law Journal*.

Fisher, L. (2015a). Presidential Unilateral Action: Constitutional and Political Checks. *Congress and the Presidency*, 42(3), 293–316.

Fisher, L. (2015b). *Presidential Spending Power*. Princeton, NJ: Princeton University Press.

Fisher, L. (2016). The Staying Power of Erroneous Dicta from Curtis-Wright to Zivotofsky. *Constitutional Comment*, 31(14), 149–219.

Fisher, L. (2017). *Supreme Court Expansion of Presidential Power: Unconstitutional Leanings*. Lawrence, KS: University Press of Kansas.

Gaziano, T. (2001). *The Use and Abuse of Executive Orders and Other Presidential Directives*. Washington, DC: Heritage Foundation.

Hamilton, A. (1987). Federalist No. 70. In I. Kramnick ed., *The Federalist Papers*. London: Penguin.

House of Representatives. (1952). *The Steel Seizure Case*. H. Doc. No. 534. Part 1. 82nd Congress, 2nd session.

Howell, W. (2005). Unilateral Power: A Brief Overview. *Presidential Studies Quarterly*, 35(3), 417–439.

Kagan, E. (2001). Presidential Administration. *Harvard Law Review*, 114(8), 2245–2385.

Kennedy, J. (2018). The Limits of Presidential Influence. *Journal of Political History*, 30(1), 1–24.

Lessig, L. & Sunstein, C. (1994). The President and the Administration. *Columbia Law Review*, 94(1), 2–133.

Lowande, K. & Rogowski, J. (2021). Presidential Unilateral Power. *Annual Review of Political Science*, 24, 21–43.

McDonald, F. (1994). *The American Presidency: An Intellectual History*. Lawrence, KS: University Press of Kansas.

McGarity, T. (1986). Regulatory Reform in the Reagan Era. *Maryland Law Review*, 45(2), 253–271.

Moe, T. M. & Howell, W. G. (1999). Unilateral Action and Presidential Power: A Theory. *Presidential Studies Quarterly*, 29(4), 850–873.

Morgan, E. & Barsa, M. (2020). Presidential Administration, the Appearance of Corruption, and the Rule of Law: Can Courts Rein in Unlawful Executive Orders? *Marquette Law Review*, 104(2), 285–349.

National Association of Attorneys General (2023). State Litigation and AG Activities Database. https://attorneysgeneral.org.

New Civil Liberties Alliance. (2021). Dazed and Abused: Biden's 100-Day Avalanche of Administrative Abuses. https://nclalegal.org/biden-executive-orders/.

Nolette, P. & Provost, C. (2018). Change and Continuity in the Role of State Attorneys General in the Obama and Trump Administrations. *Publius*, 48(3), 469–494.

Obama, B. (2014). Fixing the System: President Obama Is Taking Action on Immigration. Online video clip. https://obamawhitehouse.archives.gov/issues/immigration/immigration-action.

Olson, T. (1983, September 7). Memo to Edward Schmults. RRL, WHORM Subject Files, FE 003 (Executive Orders), Box 8, [FE003 (170000–294999)], #179187.

Olson, W. J. & Woll, A. (1999). Executive Orders and National Emergencies: How Presidents Have come to "Run the Country" by Usurping Legislative Power. *Policy Analysis*, 358, 1–23.

Relyea, H. (1974). *A Brief History of the Emergency Powers in the United States*. Washington, DC: U. S. Government Printing Office.

Relyea, H. (2008). *Presidential Directives: Background and Overview*. Washington, DC: Congressional Research Service.

Robertson, C., Winkelman, D. A., Bergstrand, K., and Modzelewski, D. (2016). The Appearance and the Reality of Quid Pro Quo Corruption: An Empirical Analysis. *Journal of Legal Analysis*, 8(2), 375–438.

Rohr, J. A. (1986). *To Run a Constitution: The Legitimacy of the Administrative State*. Lawrence, KS: University of Kansas press.

Rosenfeld, M. (2001). The Rule of Law and the Legitimacy of Constitutional Democracy. *California Law Review*, 74(5), 1307–1351.

Rudalevige, A. (2021). *By Executive Order: Bureaucratic Management and the Limits of Presidential Power*. Princeton, NJ: Princeton University Press.

Silvia, C. (2018) Evaluating Collaboration: The Solution to One Problem Often Causes Another. *Public Administration Review*, 78(3), 472–478.

Stack, K. (2015). An Administrative Jurisprudence: The Rule of Law in the Administrative State. *Columbia Law Review*, 115(5), 1985–2015.

Sterling, J. (2000). Above the Law: Evolution of Executive Orders. *University of West Los Angeles Law Review*, 31(1), 99–121.

Strauss, P. & Sunstein, C. (1986). The Role of the President and OMB in Informal Rulemaking. *Administrative Law Review*, 38(2), 181–206.

The White House.(2021). Fact Sheet: App. In *American Lung Association v. EPA*. No. 19–1140(CADC) 2076.

The White House. (2022, August 24). President Biden Announces Student Loan Relief Program for Borrowers Who Need It Most. https://bit.ly/3wFdbzg.

US Department of Justice. (2019). Brief for Petitioners in *Trump* v. *Sierra Club*.

Wharton, F. (1849). *State Trials of the United States during the Administrations of Washington and Adams*. Philadelphia, PA: Carey and Hart.

Wise, Charles R. (1993). Public Administration Is Constitutional and Legitimate. *Public Administration Review*, 53(3), 257–261.

Cambridge Elements ☰

Public and Nonprofit Administration

Andrew Whitford
University of Georgia
Andrew Whitford is Alexander M. Crenshaw Professor of Public Policy in the School of Public and International Affairs at the University of Georgia. His research centers on strategy and innovation in public policy and organization studies.

Robert Christensen
Brigham Young University
Robert Christensen is Professor and George Romney Research Fellow in the Marriott School at Brigham Young University. His research focuses on prosocial and antisocial behaviors and attitudes in public and nonprofit organizations.

About the Series
The foundation of this series are cutting-edge contributions on emerging topics and definitive reviews of keystone topics in public and nonprofit administration, especially those that lack longer treatment in textbook or other formats. Among keystone topics of interest for scholars and practitioners of public and nonprofit administration, it covers public management, public budgeting and finance, nonprofit studies, and the interstitial space between the public and nonprofit sectors, along with theoretical and methodological contributions, including quantitative, qualitative and mixed-methods pieces.

The Public Management Research Association
The Public Management Research Association improves public governance by advancing research on public organizations, strengthening links among interdisciplinary scholars, and furthering professional and academic opportunities in public management.

Cambridge Elements ☰

Public and Nonprofit Administration

Printed in the United States
by Baker & Taylor Publisher Services